The Professional Years

BRASSEUR

& EISLER

The Professional Years

As told to
Lynda D. Prouse

Macmillan Canada
Toronto

Canadian Cataloguing in Publication Data

Brasseur, Isabelle, 1970–
Brasseur and Eisler : the professional years

Includes index.
ISBN 0-7715-7670-6

1. Brasseur, Isabelle, 1970–   . 2. Eisler, Lloyd, 1963–   .
3. Skaters – Canada – Biography.
4. Skating – Canada.   I. Prouse, Lynda, 1951–   .
II. Eisler, Lloyd, 1963–   .   III. Title.

GV850.A2B727 1999   796.91'2'092271   C99–931419–X

This book is available at special discounts for bulk purchases by your group or organization for sales promotions, premiums, fundraising and seminars. For details, contact: CDG Books Canada, Special Sales Department, 99 Yorkville Avenue, Suite 400, Toronto, ON M5R 3K5. Tel: 416-963-8830

Jacket and interior design: Gord Robertson
Jacket photo: Marc Evon

Macmillan Canada
An imprint of CDG Books Canada Inc.
Toronto

1 2 3 4 5   FP   03 02 01 00 99

Printed in Canada

To my skating life. As I'm almost ready to move on to the next chapter in my life, this book will provide great memories.

ISABELLE

———————

To my family and friends, who have been there to guide me down this path and keep me between the lines. May I never forget to thank every one of you before the path ends.

LLOYD

———————

To my mother, Vera Prouse. You have always listened to me, comforted me and supported everything I have taken on. A more perfect mother could never be found. And to the memory of my father, Bob Prouse, who has always been my inspiration in life.

LYNDA

ACKNOWLEDGEMENTS

Throughout the years, skating has given me much, but especially many wonderful friends: Josée and Eric, who will always be there, and Lloyd, whose partnership and friendship are very dear to me. Skating has also allowed me to meet my husband, Rocky, who I want to thank for being there constantly in the last four years and for being so loving and understanding. Thank you to my family for loving me just as I am. And thank you to Lynda for writing this book. You understood what we wanted to say and did a great job in putting those feelings on paper. Lloyd and I may not always share the same opinions, but you let each of us tell our story separately and in our own way.

ISABELLE

I would like to thank the fans for their continued support over the years. You have always been there to give me a reason to want to become better. Remember, all journeys are better when shared with a true friend. Thanks, "Freddie".

LLOYD

Thank you to my husband, David Szabo, for his patience, love, understanding and support. To my sister, Marlene Dick, whose friendship and laughter I treasure. To Michael Rosenberg for his wise and caring advice. To Lou-Anne Brosseau for answering my many questions and accommodating me always. To Robert Harris and Anna Stancer—publisher and editor beyond compare. And to Isabelle and Lloyd, who opened the door and welcomed me in.

LYNDA

CONTENTS

World Professional Figure Skating Championships

Landover, Maryland – December 1994

T HE ARENA was blacked out and Isabelle stood alone on the ice. As the first notes of music played, a spotlight formed a circle around the petite pairs skater. Dressed like a man, with a handlebar moustache, bowler hat, and suit, she began to skate.

Suddenly, another light pierced the darkness. Perched on the boards, in glittering sequins and a pink boa, was Lloyd—Isabelle's partner, one-time boyfriend, and best friend. As the audience laughed at discovering the skater in women's attire and a blonde wig, he slid gracefully to the ice.

Suggestively bumping and grinding his way over to Isabelle, Lloyd tossed the boa aside and the pair clasped hands. The duo then began the artistic portion of a show that would display both amazing technical and creative ability.

The crowd gasped as the pair performed dangerous lifts and throws, sighing in relief as each daring element was completed flawlessly. There was no doubt, this couple was a favorite with the audience.

The number ended with Isabelle sitting on Lloyd's knee. Although his face was heavily made-up, it glistened with perspiration. As they bowed, Isabelle's eyes shone and she returned her partner's broad smile. This pair loved to entertain and it showed.

Thunderous applause reverberated throughout the arena as Brasseur and Eisler skated off the ice to await their marks. "They certainly have the crowd on their side," commentator Sandra Bezic remarked. Yet Lloyd looked unusually tense. It had been a long and difficult few months. Professional figure skating was not what they thought it would be.

Five-time Canadian champions, two-time Olympic bronze medalists, and World champions, the pairs couple had recently retired as amateurs. Isabelle and Lloyd's seven years together had not been easy. Often challenging the rigid skating hierarchy, their climb to the top had been peppered with frustration and controversy. When they turned professional, Isabelle and Lloyd had looked forward to skating in an environment where political issues were no longer relevant. However, they quickly discovered a whole new level of politics at play.

It seemed to take the judges forever to grade the pair. They were competing with the Russian balletic styles of Gordeeva and Grinkov and Bechke and Petrov. It was like comparing apples to oranges, but with the traditional lot of judges on this panel, it was easy to guess which team was going to be favored. As the marks appeared that would result in the couple placing third out of four teams, Lloyd blew a playful kiss to the viewing audience. Then, in an act of defiance, he flipped his arm to the judges. Their longtime coach, Josée Picard, stood to one side with a look of exasperation on her face.

When asked for their reaction to the scores, Lloyd put his hand on Isabelle's shoulder and calmly replied, "It is the same crap we put up with in amateur skating . . . this was supposed to be an artistic program and what they (the judges) are looking for, I am not really sure."

The interviewer turned to Isabelle and said, "Your first year as pros—how are you feeling about this?"

"It is hard sometimes," Isabelle answered with an unfamiliar edge to her voice. "Just because we are not used to it . . . we thought by turning pro, it would be different."

They thanked the interviewer and the television cameras moved on to the next pairs couple, but Isabelle and Lloyd didn't stay to watch. They turned away from the judges, media, and fans, disappearing down the tunnel that led backstage. What everyone didn't know was that the team that had just brought 15,000 people to their feet was very close to quitting. Brasseur and Eisler had had enough.

CHAPTER ONE

Turning Pro

Isabelle

I was miserable. Skating professionally was nothing like I expected it to be, and by the end of the first four months, it was more than I could bear. Away from home for most of the time, I was tired of life on the road. I didn't want to train anymore, and learning new tricks and numbers sparked no interest. Practicing our repertoire of throws and jumps left me irritated, and above all, I was fed up with competing. Something had to change. If it didn't, I was ready to walk away from the sport that had defined my life for as I long as I could remember.

It hadn't started out like this. When Lloyd and I announced our retirement from amateur skating in July 1994, I was looking forward to joining the professional ranks the following September. Satisfied that I had done my best and confident that nothing further could be accomplished by us at the eligible level (we were no longer eligible to compete at future Olympics), I was happy to be finished.

That July the only thing on my mind was the month and a half vacation we had promised ourselves. This time away from the rink was going to be a treat for me. The rigors of training for international amateur competition had never allowed for more than two weeks off during the summer and I was planning to take full advantage of my newfound freedom.

As glad as I was to be leaving (amateur skating), I realized Lloyd was experiencing mixed feelings. He was seven years older than me and had been competing on the national and world stage for much longer than I had. Although I was certain that the time was right to do this, I knew our departure from the eligible scene wouldn't be easy for him.

We made the formal announcement at a press conference in Toronto, surrounded by friends and family. I was feeling very calm, and answered questions from reporters with relative ease. However, when I glanced over at Lloyd, I noticed tears in his eyes and saw that he was choked up. Lloyd was my partner and best friend, and I honestly felt sorry for what he must be going through. But as for me, there were absolutely no regrets.

Lloyd

As much as anybody will tell you differently, I was ready to quit amateur skating. It's true that Isabelle wanted to leave a couple of years earlier than I did, but she stuck it out for me. Our goals hadn't been fully realized and I thought that two more years in the eligible ranks would afford us the time to achieve them. It did, and I am grateful to Isabelle for giving me that opportunity. However, I had no idea how difficult it would be when the time to say goodbye actually arrived. I had thought we would announce our retirement from amateur skating at the press conference, answer a few questions, and make our exit. What I hadn't counted on was becoming so emotional.

It suddenly occurred to me that I wasn't just turning away from the hard work, politics, and regulations of the sport, which I had been eager to do. I was also leaving the only world I had ever known, and it was a hell of a lot harder than I had imagined. I had loved that environment. It was structured and orderly, and I knew what was expected of me on a day-to-day basis. The notoriety that came with winning medals for Canada was also immensely gratifying. I was particularly going to miss competing at the eligible level; preparing for competitions and striving to be number one was something that always fully engaged me. Now it was all going to change, I realized, and for the first time since we had decided to retire, the uncertainty of my future frightened me.

Not having a chance to say goodbye to our fans also upset me. They had stood by us since the beginning of our career. I even knew many of them by name. Of course, I didn't realize then how visible Isabelle and I would become once we started skating professionally. In fact, both of us were unaware what this career change would entail. Unfortunately, the ignorance we shared almost led to our downfall a few months later.

Isabelle

The summer of 1994 passed all too quickly. The six weeks I took off gave my body a chance to heal from the grueling wear placed on it the previous season. Because I wasn't as strong as Lloyd, I used to have to train very hard just to keep up with him on the ice. Now I didn't have to train for five hours a day and it was such a relief. I even had time for the surgery I needed to repair a deviated septum that had bothered me for a while.

My fondest memories of that summer were the ones spent on the boat I purchased. Along with my mother and brother, I wiled away the hours on the waters of Quebec, where the furthest thing from my mind was a cold ice rink and a pair of skates. Since the passing of my father two years earlier, I felt a strong need to be with my family and I cherished the moments with them. However, as precious as that time was to me, by late August I was feeling lost.

I missed skating. When friends asked me what my plans were for the fall, I couldn't answer. This concerned me. Since childhood, each day of my life had been meticulously planned, and when I was training for the Olympics, my schedule was laid out by the hour. If I wasn't skating, I was at the gym or planning programs with my choreographer and coach. Every aspect of my life had revolved around competing. Too much free time loomed before me now and I wasn't accustomed to it.

When we turned professional, or ineligible, as our status is now referred to, it never entered my mind that skating would become a full-time job. I thought our appearances would be limited, and that we would be skating just for fun. The time away from the rink that I had longed for in July was now making me anxious. Just because I had wanted to escape the disciplined training of the eligible world didn't mean that I had lost my feeling for the sport. Even though the last few years had been a physical strain, I still loved skating, and found myself looking more forward than usual to appearing with Lloyd in our only scheduled show of the new season.

Lloyd

At the beginning of the summer, all Isabelle and I knew for sure was that we would be back on the Tom Collins Champions on Ice tour the following spring. Dreams on Ice, the show Isabelle and I had produced and starred in since 1992, was set for early September; other than that, no skating events were on our calendar. I hoped that over the next few months promoters and organizers would learn of our availability and invite us to their shows and competitions.

I passed the summer determined not to worry. I made long-overdue visits to family and friends and enjoyed my time off. Although Isabelle and I were both living in Montreal, our paths didn't cross much, but on the few occasions that we did speak, my partner assured me she was relaxing.

It was a well-deserved rest for Isabelle. In spite of a cracked rib, she had persevered through the Olympics, World Championships, and then the Tom Collins Tour, and I don't think I had ever been prouder of her. The two of us had endured many hardships over the course of our careers, and I have always admired my partner's courage. But the fortitude Isabelle displayed at the 1994 Worlds astonished me. In that kind of pain, most skaters would have withdrawn from the competition. But not Isabelle. She had certainly earned this vacation from skating.

Isabelle

It was our second year of staging Dreams on Ice, a charity show Lloyd, Lou-Anne Brosseau, and I produce to benefit the Children's Wish Foundation. We invite amateur and professional skaters alike to participate in the show, and although it was great being back on the ice, it also felt strange. For the first time since pairing up in 1987, Lloyd and I weren't really prepared; we'd only skated together for a few days prior to the show. Normally, we returned to training as a team at least a month before the start of the season. Most of the other skaters participating in the show couldn't believe we were actually ready to perform before an audience with so little training time. To tell you the truth, I wondered myself. But luckily we skated well, using exhibition routines from the previous season.

During rehearsals, I listened to younger skaters discuss the upcoming season, and was relieved that the endless competing and ongoing training would be just a memory to Lloyd and me. We had already proven ourselves; never once did it occur to me that I would have to go back to practicing the throws, jumps, and other elements that were required in the eligible (skating) world. Although we had recently been asked to appear in a few shows and competitions, I thought everything would be easy from now on. Traveling would be at a minimum and if I wanted a day off, I assumed I would just take it. That September, I happily, and wrongly, believed all the nerve-racking aspects of skating were behind me.

Lloyd

As coproducer of Dreams on Ice, I had a lot to keep me occupied, including our own performance. In preparation of the show, we hadn't trained as hard as we normally did. Although we skated admirably, I knew that if we were to be back in top competitive form for the season, we would have to begin training almost immediately after the show. Assuming that Isabelle realized this, I didn't discuss it with her in any depth. She was healthy now, and it was time to get on with our skating.

The International Management Group (IMG), who represented us, had brought offers for a number of competitions, including the Canadian Professional Championships, the World Professional Figure Skating Championships, and the Challenge of Champions. My anxiety about being invited to various events apparently had been groundless, because we had been asked to participate in almost all of the professional competitions that fall.

Over the next four months, the offers kept coming and because of our initial insecurity at being asked, and our desire to make a name for ourselves in the professional skating world, we agreed to everything. This sat well with me, and I was eager to participate in the various events. I have always thrived on pressure, and I found my new life to be very exciting. Being accepted into this realm was important to our careers, and if it meant taking every offer that came our way, so be it.

I never thought about the earning potential of accepting so many appearances. Money has never been my motivation to skate. There are some skaters who grab at every opportunity to perform, and their main purpose is to receive a paycheck. They joke about their million-dollar homes and the way their various appearances support their extravagant lifestyles. A few have even dubbed themselves "tour whores." The majority of skaters, however, are like Isabelle and me. They work hard because they have a passion to skate and perform.

Isabelle

Since Lloyd and I were so inexperienced, we were afraid to turn down any offers. And in the beginning, it almost drove me crazy. As much as I began to dread our frequent appearances, it was obvious that Lloyd was happy to be skating so much.

Neither of us ever thought about the money we could make. Later, however, when I was struggling to adapt to the pressures of skating professionally, I did use the idea of making money to help me through.

When I was skating at the amateur level, there were always goals to meet. Without those goals, I soon found myself floundering. I couldn't relate to the hype of professional competitions, since winning them didn't seem so important to me. To me there was no comparison between these events and amateur competitions. To help keep myself focused and motivated, I made up my own goals. For example, I would promise myself certain items for the house I had recently bought, if I landed a difficult throw or jump in competition. I came to look upon skating as a job, and giving myself a reward was an incentive to work hard and skate well. It was no different than when I was a child and my dad promised me a puppy if I landed certain jumps. I practiced for hours, mastered the jumps, and received the dog. I used this method only through that initial season. As I eventually came to terms with skating professionally, I was able to put that way of thinking aside. In those first dismal months, however, the approach helped.

Lloyd

We debuted as professional competitors in early October at the North American Open. This was a one-time-only event, held at the new Gund Arena in Cleveland. Areas of the building were still uncompleted, and I noticed that the ice was in particularly bad shape. However, I assumed it would be brought up to par for the competition.

I had been complaining all week about my skate blades. Unlike many skaters, I don't have any routine when it comes to sharpening them, other than I usually try to have the procedure done before coming to a competition. This time I didn't, however, and after having them sharpened in Cleveland, the blades just didn't feel right. I had them sharpened twice more before the competition, but I was still uncomfortable skating on them.

We were informed that technical and artistic programs were required for the competition, but we were left in the dark as to the specifics. Professional competitions were still in their infancy; rules were sketchy and undefined. Even those who had been skating professionally for a few years had trouble figuring out what the judges wanted.

Since we didn't know what the officials expected, Isabelle and I decided to repeat two proven programs from our amateur portfolio. We skated the technical portion to "Theme on Paganini," our winning program from the 1993 World Championships, while our comedic routine, which is usually referred to as the "Lady and the Man" number, seemed ideal for the artistic portion. This exhibition piece, in which Isabelle and I cross-dress, had always received an enthusiastic response whenever it was performed.

We performed the technical number first, and when we stepped on the ice for warm-up, I noticed again how atrocious the surface was. I soon discovered that it was this way for almost all professional competitions. Most organizers don't appear to care about the condition of the ice. With ticket sales being their main concern, flaws on the ice, which can be damaging to programs, as well as to skaters, are shockingly low on the priority list.

We were the first to compete, and right from the beginning our performance was not up to our usual standards; we skated awful. Isabelle fell on a throw triple Salchow, and ten seconds later we crashed on a lift that has been documented many times over. This was the only time Isabelle and I have ever fallen on a lift, including in practice. It was unfortunate that the fall occurred during our professional debut.

After recovering from the first fall, we were skating down the ice, preparing ourselves for the Brasseur/Eisler Star Lift. I put the lift up, and as Isabelle ascended into the air, I caught the left outside edge of my blade and went down. Whether it was the poor ice surface, the fact that my blades didn't feel right, or a combination of the two, I have no idea. But from that moment on, everything seemed to be moving in slow motion. I felt myself dropping, but also saw that Isabelle was falling—headfirst. Instinct kicked in and I thought: protect her head. In pairs, we are taught that we must save the girl from any injury, especially to the head. Lying on the ice, I lifted my left arm and somehow caught Isabelle under the chin. As she tumbled down, her head stayed up but she landed hard on her elbows and knees.

Getting to my feet, I felt pain in my knee but I was far more concerned about Isabelle. "Are you all right?" I asked frantically.

"Yeah, yeah," she answered. "Just keep going."

Relieved that Isabelle appeared to have come out of the fall fairly unscathed, I began to skate; however, my knee was aching. Isabelle noticed my discomfort and asked me if I wanted to stop, but we both knew that wouldn't happen. Isabelle and I had skated through much worse in the past, and short of something very serious, we weren't the type of skaters to quit in the middle of a number.

I finished the program in a daze. In all my years of skating, with four different partners, I had never fallen on a lift like that and it had shaken me up.

We stepped off the ice, and while waiting for our marks in the kiss-and-cry area, the fall was replayed on the Jumbotron, amid gasps from the audience. I later learned that it was also repeated on every television set in North America that had tuned in to the event. Fans and media alike were as stunned as Isabelle and I. Something like this just didn't happen to the team of Brasseur and Eisler.

Our marks came up and were, deservedly, low. We placed dead last against Gordeeva and Grinkov and Bechke and Petrov, in the technical part of the program. What really threw me, though, was the horde of reporters that pounced on Isabelle and me as we limped our way backstage. Everyone wanted interviews but we were in no mood. Huge bruises were beginning to appear on Isabelle's arms and legs. And my knee, which had recently undergone surgery, was throbbing. I just wanted to get back to the dressing room, have Isabelle checked out, and put some ice on my knee.

Isabelle

As I began to fall, I wasn't sure what was going on. After skating with Lloyd for so many years and having not had anything like this occur before, it all seemed dreamlike. It happened fast, but in my mind, the fall seemed to take so long. One second my partner was holding me in the air, and the next, I couldn't feel him under me.

I don't remember Lloyd protecting my head, yet when I watched the videotape afterwards, I saw that he clearly did. What I do recall was my own worry about kicking my partner with the blade of my skate as I came down. To avoid this, I bent my feet back before hitting the ice, which is also apparent on the videotape. In pairs skating, you don't think about yourself—at least Lloyd and I don't. We try to protect our partner first, and then ourselves.

We had been fairly fortunate up to that point. The only other time I remember us having a close call was during a move we call the Hydrant; in this move, I am thrown over Lloyd's head in a split position. As I was going over, my foot got tangled in his outfit and I started coming down headfirst. Thank goodness I was wearing a skirt that day, because Lloyd was able to catch me by the garment. The skirt ripped but he stopped the fall with my face only an inch away from the ice.

In an interview we gave after the mishap in Cleveland, I admitted that I was nervous about trying the Star Lift again. Once we returned home, however, we knew we had to perform it immediately. If we put it off, it would become increasingly difficult for me to confront the move.

On our first day back at the rink in Boucherville, Quebec, where we trained, we warmed up by stroking around the ice. Then, without saying a word, I took off my gloves and laid them down. Since we don't practice lifts with gloves on, because we require the hand-to-hand contact, it was a sign to my partner that I wanted to give the lift a try. Lloyd looked at me and asked, "Are you ready?"

Our coach, Josée, was standing nearby and asked me what we were talking about. When I told her we were going to attempt the Star Lift, her eyes widened and she said, "I'll be back in five minutes." Josée had been with us in Cleveland, had seen the fall, and now couldn't bear to watch. As soon as she left, we went into the lift, successfully completed it, then carried on with the rest of our practice. I felt much better. It was like falling from a horse. I just had to face my fear and get right back up there.

Lloyd

With the injuries we had sustained after the fall in Cleveland, we didn't know if we would be able to finish the competition. My knee was sore and Isabelle had bruises the size of baseballs on her elbows and legs. Since both of us hated the idea of pulling out of the competition, however, we decided to proceed with a little more caution than usual.

Because we had come last in the technical part of the program, we were up first for the artistic segment. I think we surprised many people when we appeared on the ice. Injuries aside, we skated our best and received almost all-perfect scores. We won the artistic program and moved to second place overall. It would be the only time we would beat Gordeeva and Grinkov in any component of professional skating. It is interesting to note that when we skated that same number—again flawlessly—a couple of months later at the World Professional Skating Championships, our marks were at the other end of the spectrum.

Isabelle

Early on in our professional career, we decided that we would still work with our coaches. Eric Gillies and Josée had been with us every step of the way in our amateur careers, and although we didn't train with them the same way we used to, they continued to provide us with valuable input.

It wasn't easy for any of us that first season. Since Josée and Eric were used to amateur skaters, it took them a while to become accustomed to what we were doing. As professionals, we would often be required to compete within the week, with very little training. This was unheard of by our coaches, whose skaters had months to train for one competition, and who were on a rigid daily schedule. Josée and Eric rightly believed that if we were going to participate in so many competitions, we should be more disciplined in our training. The problem was, I didn't want to practice at that level of intensity anymore, which caused friction between me and Lloyd.

Lloyd knew all along that we had to continue training. He was ready to work hard for his professional career, but I wasn't. I didn't understand why we had to. I would arrive at the rink grumpy, and as we got into our session, I would begin to complain. I didn't want to practice throws and jumps. As far as I was concerned, the grinding workouts were unnecessary. Perturbed by my behavior, Lloyd would ask what it was I wanted to do. I couldn't answer him, because I just didn't know.

Practicing our show numbers, on the other hand, was a pleasure. They were fun and didn't require side-by-side jumps and throw triple Salchows. Performing these routines is what I thought we would be doing as pros. However, as we accepted invitations to more and more competitions, it became apparent that I would have to start practicing and performing the same elements I used to dread as an amateur. My obvious reluctance to do so strained my relationship with Lloyd.

Little by little, we all adjusted. We had to. When we compete now, our coaches still play a part. Josée has attended many of our professional competitions and I always find her presence to be most comforting. She is completely in tune with our personalities, and is able to diffuse many of the stresses that come with competing. However, it took months before we were all able to fully understand and adapt to this new life.

Lloyd

Josée and Eric continued to give us the time we needed, but because we were on the road so much, it was almost impossible to train on a regular basis. For every three days we were at home, we would be away four. If a competition or show happened to take place on a Wednesday, we would have to travel on either the previous Sunday or Monday. This would ensure enough practice time at the venue, and also allow us the hours to take care of promotion and interviews. Usually tired after a competition, we wouldn't return home until the following day. It was all so new to us that we just didn't know how to schedule ourselves.

I realized Isabelle was getting edgy about having no personal time, but our constant traveling didn't bother me at all. I was pleased we were in such demand and thought Isabelle would come around when she got used to our new lifestyle. In the meantime, I believed that in our free time we should be training or creating new programs. The trouble was, Isabelle wanted no part of it.

We had been accustomed to skating daily when we were amateurs, and frequently it was me who wanted to skip training. Isabelle used to insist that we keep on schedule. If I didn't show up for practice, she would even come to my apartment and demand that I follow her to the rink. Now our roles had reversed. I was the one who was pushing, while she was reluctant to work. Isabelle believed that by turning professional she wouldn't have to skate daily or work out so much. As we were soon to discover, professional skating was far more arduous than amateur skating. When Isabelle realized that, it became a struggle between us: I wanted to skate as much as I could and Isabelle didn't, which created an increasingly stressful situation for both of us.

Isabelle

It was all so frustrating. I had turned professional to get away from hard work and travel, and now there seemed to be more than ever. I was constantly in conflict with myself, because deep down I knew I should be training. When I wasn't skating regularly, visiting the gym, and eating nutritionally, everything was more difficult for me on the ice. Aside from not wanting to train as hard, I didn't see how it was possible anyway. We were constantly traveling, and when we were at home, training was haphazard and not what I was accustomed to.

If I was going to continue in this fashion, I at least needed some sort of planned agenda. I hated not knowing where I would be from week to week, and the lack of structure in my life was playing havoc with my nerves.

I found all the traveling we did most stressful. When I purchased my home in September, I thought I would be around long enough to enjoy it. That, however, was not to be. Visions of decorating the house, and being there with my family, rapidly disappeared as I spent more and more time in hotels and airplanes. It was a dream I had to put by the wayside.

Other factors contributed to my anguish. Back then, I was dating Jean-Luc Brassard, who had won a gold medal in mogul skiing at the 1994 Olympics. Jean-Luc was as busy as I was, with commitments that are naturally attached to being an Olympic champion, and from September until Christmas, we only saw each other twice. This situation did not help strengthen our relationship, and was another reason I was fast growing impatient with my harried lifestyle.

Moreover, I had signed up for four courses during the summer in order to finish college. I had postponed completing my education the previous year because I was training for the Olympics, and I was now determined to obtain my degree. I actually believed I could attend school with the rest of the students. In fact, I was forced to take the courses by correspondence.

I had expected to lead a more normal life now that I was out of the eligible ranks, and it wasn't happening. At that point, I was convinced that skating was standing in the way of my happiness—something I had never felt as an amateur.

Lloyd

I probably should have paid more attention to what Isabelle was going through. She repeatedly complained about the increasingly hectic schedule and the constant traveling we had to do to get to competitions and shows.

The traveling didn't bother me. Since I wasn't dating anyone in particular that fall and had no other commitments, my focus was on skating and trying to establish ourselves professionally. What I did have a problem with was that we were going from one competition to the next, without knowing what was expected of us. Trying to figure out what the judges wanted from our performances was a constant source of aggravation.

At that stage of professional skating there were only guidelines, and we quickly learned that competition marks could be affected by what appeared to be arbitrary factors: on whether or not the judges liked your hair, your skating outfit, or the music you selected. It seemed that you could skate a perfect program, but if they were unimpressed by the color of your costume or the rhythm of your music, you could easily be delegated to last place.

Isabelle and I never knew for sure if we were making the right decisions, as we attempted to develop new programs for the various competitions. Certainly Josée and Eric helped us out whenever they could, but we weren't home all that much, and besides, they had their regular students to look after. Turning to any of the other pairs skaters on the professional circuit was out of the question as well. Although most of us were friends, we were also competitors, and I didn't expect them to share their secrets with us. Isabelle and I were the new kids on the block and we would just have to learn for ourselves.

Nowhere did it become more apparent that the judges could love us one moment and hate us the next than at the 1994 World Professional Figure Skating Championships in December. A few weeks earlier, we had won the artistic part of a competition with our "Lady and the Man" number and had received perfect sixes from most of the judges. At the World Professional Championships, we skated the same number in almost the exact fashion. There, we received a standing ovation from the audience, yet the judges disapproved. We came dead last.

No matter how confusing it was trying to figure out what the judges wanted, I always believed, and still do, that the most important judge was the audience. I·had assumed that the entertainment aspect would be stepped up for professional skating, but again, I was mistaken. The judges' apparent lack of sensibility so frustrated me that, in a moment of anger, I flipped my arm to them. It wasn't only their tunnel vision that annoyed me. My gesture came after I'd had to put up with poor ice, bad lighting, and total disorganization. I was upset with the entire production, as a matter of fact. It had been a week of disarray, with one screw-up after another. The judges' low opinion of our performance was just the final blow.

It would take us three years before we agreed to do the World Professional Championships again. In the meantime, I was fed up with professional skating in general. Between my animosity and the escalated arguing between Isabelle and me, I had almost reached my limit.

Isabelle

When Lloyd flipped his arm to the judges, I thought, Oh, oh, here we go again. I always back him up but sometimes I don't understand why he does things like that. In my opinion, we had skated well and the audience had loved the number. If the judges didn't like it, what can you do? However, that is Lloyd's personality and it didn't change just because we had turned professional. I, too, was upset at the way that competition, like many others, was run. By then, however, I didn't care as much as I should have, as I was rapidly losing my interest in professional skating.

A couple of weeks later, Lloyd and I were at a training center in Simsbury, Connecticut. We had been there a few days, when I told Lloyd that I didn't want to take on so much in the future. I had been home only a week or two since September and I needed a rest. Lloyd told me there wasn't much we could do about our full calendar because we had already signed contracts; we didn't have a choice, he informed me.

"Well, *I* have a choice," I replied angrily. "I can just stop skating."

Lloyd paused a second before he answered, "If that's what you want, then do it."

At that moment, I wasn't certain if quitting skating was what I truly wanted, but I did know that I had been pushed to the edge and I had to do something about it.

"Fine," I said. "I had a great career with you, but now it's over. If you still want to be friends, you know where to reach me." Then I grabbed my things, called a cab, and left for the airport.

When I arrived home, I took a few days to think things through and, deciding I needed some professional advice, I paid a visit to Dr. Peter Jensen, the sports psychologist who had helped Lloyd and me get over some tough times in our amateur career. Dr. Jensen told me that my reasons for quitting skating and leaving my partner weren't good enough. He emphasized that Lloyd and I had very different personalities from each other and for the past four months we had been going in opposite directions. Lloyd had been ready to devote 100 percent into developing our new careers, while I hadn't been ready to put my all into it. Dr. Jensen suggested that Lloyd and I talk to each other and set goals. Furthermore, he recommended that we write everything down. His advice made a lot of sense. I realized that I couldn't let skating—and Lloyd—go, just like that, so I decided to give it one more try.

Before I left Simsbury, I told Lloyd that I would honor my commitment to perform in the Ice Capades in Montreal, from Christmas to New Year's. We had done the show annually for a number of years, and I just couldn't back out of it. In between performances, Lloyd and I sat down and followed Dr. Jensen's advice. For the first time since we had turned professional, we really talked and put everything down on paper, including a list of my needs and expectations. Lloyd agreed to cut back on our skating, while I promised to take things a little more seriously and to let him know when I was getting upset. I also had some time off in February after injuring my shoulder, and I am sure that being at home for a couple of weeks helped to improve my mood as well.

Lloyd

In November and December, Isabelle and I weren't getting along. She was always crying and saying how much she hated professional skating and being on the road. She also missed her family terribly when she was away. Ever since her father's death, Isabelle seemed to have an emotional need to be physically close to her brother and mother.

It took us months to get to the root of the problem, since neither of us could put our finger on what exactly was wrong. The result was that we argued about everything. For example, Isabelle would get upset, wondering why we had to travel on a Friday when the show wasn't taking place until Saturday, while I would get irritated that we weren't practicing enough. We both disliked the poorly-run competitions and sometimes arbitrary process. We couldn't agree on anything, and the slightest difference in viewpoint would set us off. Somehow we had to get past the tears and arguments and face what was really bothering us.

We had just finished a competition and had headed straight to Simsbury to train before the next event. There was more tension than usual between us, and our pent-up feelings soon surfaced. We were at the rink bickering once again over our schedule. Referring to some future event, Isabelle asked, "Why did you accept this?" Then she firmly stated that she didn't want to do it.

"You should have said something when the offer came in," I shot back, exasperated.

"You know I have a hard time saying no," she replied.

We quibbled back and forth for a few more minutes. Then, with some emotion, Isabelle announced that she wanted to quit skating.

Hurt by her outburst, I insisted she leave. "Pack up your bags and go home," I said flatly. "We'll deal with this later."

In retrospect, I should have seen it coming. We had never sat down and talked about our expectations. I had just been going along, worrying more about the competitions and how we were faring on the professional scene, while my partner was growing more discontent by the day.

Isabelle left immediately while I stayed in Simsbury. We didn't speak for a while, but I did have some long discussions with Bob Young, a good friend of mine. Bob is a noted pairs coach, as well as the director of the Simsbury rink. He had worked with Isabelle and me many times in the past and was familiar with the various problems we'd experienced. Bob suggested that Isabelle and I reconnect through frank communication, and that each of us should give the other what we needed as individuals. In that way, he said, the team would function once again as a whole entity. Bob's advice wasn't startling to me. It was something that Isabelle and I usually practiced; however, we had lost our direction over the past four months. Our failing to talk had almost destroyed the team, and the friendship, in a very short time.

The next thing I did was contact our agent, Yuki Saegusa. I told her that we had to change the way we did our scheduling and that if we didn't, Isabelle was going to quit. Except in special circumstances, there was to be no more calling us on a Monday and asking us to appear at an event the following Thursday. Our itinerary would have to be laid out in advance.

Over the next several days, I thought about where we had gone wrong and how I could change it. I drafted a rough plan for the remainder of the season and canceled some bookings, all the while hoping that Isabelle would change her mind. We didn't speak much over this period, deciding it best to leave each other alone for a while.

Isabelle and I met at the Forum in Montreal for the Ice Capades, where fourteen shows were scheduled over a five-day period. Although I was glad to have Isabelle back at my side again, I realized that we had a lot of work to do and some serious decisions to make.

The first thing we did was confirm that we both still loved skating. That was the most important element to us, because without the passion there was no point in going on. We spent hours just talking and letting each other know what was troubling each of us. I showed Isabelle the tentative schedule I'd drawn up, and by December 31, we had finally set down the guidelines on how to solve our problem. Settling on a compromise, we agreed that I was going to have to stop accepting every offer that came our way, and Isabelle was going to have to speak up as soon as something disturbed her. There was to be no more stewing in silence for either of us.

We also decided that I would be the one to refuse engagements. Isabelle has a much harder time than I turning down requests. In order to save our partnership, I took on the aggressive role. Many of the contracts I turned down offered huge amounts of money, and I'm sure our refusal to do the various events stunned a few people in the business. But as I stated earlier, money has never been an issue for either of us. Isabelle's happiness, and mine, was paramount.

I admit that if it had been left to me, I probably would have continued appearing in every event that came our way. Skating is like breathing to me. It is something that I *have* to do, and turning down opportunities to perform disturbed me in the beginning. In this sense, I believe I made the bigger sacrifice. Yet it was offered without resentment, because I knew in my heart, in order for us to continue skating, Isabelle needed this.

CHAPTER TWO

Dreams on Ice

Isabelle

THE FIRST YEAR we put Dreams on Ice together was more like a nightmare than a dream. What began as a little local show with a few friends turned into a major television production, featuring some of the world's best skaters. None of us running the event knew what we were doing, and the days leading up to the show were plagued by problems.

Lloyd and I evolved from skaters to producers as a result of an idea put to us by Lou-Anne Brosseau, our then fan club president. She worked with the Children's Wish Foundation of Canada as a volunteer, and in 1991 asked us if we were interested in acting as spokespersons for the foundation. Lloyd and I jumped at the chance for a couple of reasons: we both like being around children; and because we have been fortunate to realize many of our own dreams, we were happy to assist others in achieving theirs. What could be more gratifying than to help make a dream come true for a child suffering from a life-threatening illness? But because we were still competing at the amateur level, there never seemed to be enough time to devote to the organization. Then Lou-Anne came up with the idea to put on a show. "Do what you do best," she offered. "Skate."

Lloyd

Great concept, I thought, when I first heard Lou-Anne's proposal to mount a production. The Children's Wish Foundation needed money to grant wishes for the children and we would at last be able to contribute to the cause. Before I made a final commitment, however, I called a few friends and asked if they would be willing to participate, should the show become a reality. Everyone was enthusiastic, so we decided to go ahead. Isabelle and I would hold a little fundraiser the following September in Windsor, Ontario.

Planning for the event began immediately. First we had to come up with a name for the show. We settled on Dreams on Ice because of the obvious connection with the foundation's mandate to make dreams come true for children. I am pleased that the name has now become synonymous not only with Isabelle and me, but with the charity as well.

Christening the show was only the beginning. As Isabelle and I soon discovered, there were hundreds of details to attend to. Luckily, Lou-Anne lived in the Windsor area and was able to do a lot of the legwork that would have been impossible for Isabelle and me, considering our own harried schedules. She found a venue, sold some sponsors to come on board, and generally put the word out. Meanwhile, Isabelle and I rounded up eleven other skaters, who agreed to appear with us.

Isabelle

It wasn't as easy as we thought to book the skaters for that initial show. In fact, the entire roster changed over the course of the planning period because of injuries and other unforeseen occurrences. For instance, 1992 Canadian champion Michael Slipchuk fractured his ankle two days before the show. After some desperate phone calls, we were able to replace him with American skater Mark Mitchell.

We wanted to invite both professional and amateur skaters to participate. The cast we assembled was exceptional. Included in the inaugural performance were: Brian Orser, Jill Trenary, Elvis Stojko, Karen Preston, and Christine Hough and her partner, Doug Ladret. When Elvis skated, the crowd cheered so loud and long, he had trouble hearing his music.

Lloyd

When a television network approached us about taping the event for their fall lineup of television specials, we were delighted to accept. It would be exposure for us, the show, and the Children's Wish Foundation. However, we had no inkling of the headaches it would cause and the work it would entail.

We had appeared on camera in other people's events, but we didn't have any experience in television production. Organizing a show for the entertainment of an arena audience was one thing, and fairly routine: you come in, set up, skate, go home—no problem. With the television network involved, however, our plans changed drastically.

First the venue had to be booked for a longer period of time, because now there was equipment to be set up. Cameras and special lighting and sound systems were to be brought in on huge moving vans. The backstage corridors of the Windsor arena became a labyrinth of cables and high-tech gear. Moreover, the various systems required numerous highly skilled people to operate them. Instead of the fast-paced rehearsals that I prefer, the sessions became long and drawn-out as we worked with television producers, who weren't all that experienced in skating. To top it off, I had agreed to choreograph the opening and closing segments, and along with our music director, Denis Laframboise, who has been with us for years, I even helped to cut and edit the music.

Isabelle and I were so green, it was probably just as well that we didn't know what lay ahead. BBE Productions, the company we now own and operate to produce Dreams on Ice and other shows, wasn't even formed at that stage. Hence, this initial venture was a little like running a show out of our basements. Considering our lack of experience, it was nothing short of a miracle that we were able to pull it off.

Isabelle

Dreams on Ice was scheduled for September because that month usually wasn't a very busy time for skaters. Since then other producers and promoters have seen the benefits of staging productions in the early autumn. Consequently, it is getting increasingly difficult for us to hire talent.

Moreover, many skaters are booked a year in advance to events that pay them huge salaries that we could never match. Because Dreams on Ice is a charity show, with much of the proceeds going to the Children's Wish Foundation, skaters can't be paid as much for performing in the event as they would be for a regular appearance. Although Lloyd and I donate our own time for free, we couldn't possibly ask other skaters to do the same, just as we couldn't perform gratis for every charity event we appear in. Skaters are invited to so many functions of this kind that if we did them all for free, we wouldn't be able to survive financially.

However, many of the skaters who have performed in our show have not only agreed to skate for a lower fee, they have also donated a portion of their earnings to the foundation. Lloyd and I are grateful when this occurs and we reciprocate if they are producing, or taking part in, a charity event that is important to them. Brian Orser is one skater who has long been doing our show. He produces many charity events of his own, to raise money for various hospitals in Calgary and Toronto. And whenever he asks, Lloyd and I will skate at his events. We help him and he helps us.

Lloyd

As the industry becomes more money hungry, we are having a harder time booking skaters for our show. Every year, though, we somehow manage to come up with an impressive cast, attracting some of the most celebrated names in our sport: Brian Orser, Kurt Browning, Shae-Lynn Bourne and Victor Kraatz, Josée Chouinard, Barb Underhill and Paul Martini, Michelle Kwan, Todd Eldredge, Yuka Sato, Jozef Sabovcik, Nancy Kerrigan, Kristi Yamaguchi, Rocky Marval, Calla Urbanski, Paul Wylie, and Elvis Stojko have all appeared at least once in Dreams on Ice. But we don't invite people to participate just because they have a famous name. First and foremost, we invite our friends. Someone like Brian Orser truly understands why Isabelle and I have made this commitment to the foundation. Brian is always there when we need him and has appeared in six of our seven shows to date. Brian is consummately generous and one of the easiest people to work with. Unlike certain other skaters, he is not demanding and always adds a positive note to our backstage banter.

In addition to inviting our old friends to perform in the show, every year we attempt to include a new face in the lineup, as well as a top-name athlete. Obviously, the more popular the skaters are, the more tickets we will sell. I have often been asked by curious fans why we don't repeatedly book such skaters as Stojko or Bourne and Kraatz, who are sure crowd pleasers. I tell people that we would be thrilled to have these favorites appear on a regular basis. We invite them, but whether they accept or not is their choice, not ours.

Another problem we have in attracting some of the eligible skaters to Dreams on Ice is the limited budget we have to work with. This has become increasingly frustrating to me over the last couple of years, as rules soften and eligible skaters are now relatively free to skate where they want. More important, they are paid big money to appear. This change in regulations has led to an extremely disturbing idea among many of the younger skaters, who seem to believe that our sport is strictly about money. Currently there are many events that a skater can choose from in the month of September, and the promoters all pay handsomely. There is no way that our show can compete with those seductive dollars.

When I invite a younger skater to participate in Dreams on Ice and they request some ridiculous fee, it makes my blood boil. In an attempt to be patient with them, I will ask if they could possibly take half the amount, and explain that by doing so, the children will benefit. I will even point out to them that some skaters will do the show for free, as did Todd Eldredge in 1996, when he donated his earnings to the foundation. But these kids will look at me as if I am crazy and decline. It's all I can do to keep my mouth closed to stop from calling them the spoiled brats that they have become. Maybe I am too passionate about the show, but I can't understand how these very fortunate people don't have the time or inclination to give something back. It irritates me to no end.

Isabelle

There is no question that Lloyd and I care deeply about the show and the Children's Wish Foundation. We have experienced and shared heartbreaking moments with some of these children. I have especially fond memories of the first child we were able to help. Her name was Sarah and she had a rare form of leukemia. Before her illness, Sarah was a figure skater and had the same Olympic dreams that Lloyd and I once had. We arranged to bring Sarah and her family to the show and she spent the day with us. I recall the little hat she wore to cover the visible signs of the chemotherapy she was undergoing, which also left her too tired to skate.

The following year we were at the rink, participating in an event that allows the public to skate with the stars of Dreams on Ice and obtain autographs. A little girl approached me and requested my signature on a photograph. She looked at me shyly and then asked, "Don't you remember me, Isabelle?" At first, I didn't recognize her. This child had long hair and was on skates. I stared into her eyes and then it dawned on me.

"Sarah?" I exclaimed in surprise, not quite believing who I was seeing. Her treatments had been successful and the leukemia had gone into remission. She was healthy and happy, and I was grateful for the miracles of modern medicine. Unfortunately, not all the children we have met through the Children's Wish Foundation have had a happy ending.

Lloyd

There was one little girl whose wish was to meet Isabelle and me. We found it very humbling that of all the dreams she could have chosen, hers was to spend a day with us. The request came from the Children's Wish Foundation in November. Because she was so ill, we decided to see the girl while we were in Toronto, performing at the Cavalcade of Lights, an outdoor Christmas show held at Nathan Phillip's Square.

I was immensely moved by this child's bravery. We talked and ate lunch together, and she attended the show as our special guest, where her smile lit up the night sky. A few weeks later, I was saddened to learn that she had died.

When I heard the news, I began to look at life in an entirely different perspective. Suddenly, skating and winning medals seemed trivial. And I felt that way for a long time afterwards. As with any moving experience, the despondent emotions eventually faded, but they never left me completely. Sometimes, when I am overwrought at a competition, where I don't believe the judges have treated us fairly, I will stop and find myself thinking about that little girl. Everything else will pale in comparison, and instantly, the judges' marks won't seem so important after all.

Isabelle

Another of my favorite memories happened in 1995, when Elvis Stojko was skating in the show. Jocelyn was an ill teenager who wanted to meet him more than anything else in the world. We were hosting a media reception, where the skaters who were appearing in the show had gathered to talk to the press. Jocelyn was also invited, but didn't know that the skaters would be present.

Lloyd and I met her at the door, and she was overcome with shock when she saw us and the other skaters across the room. But when she realized that Elvis was there, Jocelyn began to cry. He put his arms around her in a warm and friendly hug, and later that night, presented her with roses at the show.

Most of the skaters who have participated in Dreams on Ice are like Elvis. Just by accepting our invitation in the first place, they have shown just how much they care about the children. In a weekend that can sometimes be taxing, they are generous with their free time, and are very cooperative when we ask them for favors to help the foundation.

Lloyd

Today, Dreams on Ice is run like a finely tuned machine. However, it took us years to work out the details, and in the process, we often stepped on each other's toes, which resulted in a few misunderstandings and arguments. We learned by trial and error, and eventually realized where our own strengths lay. Now Lou-Anne, Isabelle, and I have very specific jobs that begin about eight months before the actual show takes place. Although we consult with one another continually, we go about our responsibilities separately.

In January, when Isabelle and I are on tour with the Tom Collins Champions on Ice tour, we decide who we want to book for the show. In the early days, I used to pick up the telephone and call the skaters, or invite them when I saw them on tour or at an event. But the skating industry has since grown into a massive business. Everything must be done through the proper channels, which means booking the skaters through their agents. Once that is completed, I prepare and forward a contract.

Anyone who has ever dealt with an agent knows that they operate on a different time system than the rest of the world. Without a firm stance, they could leave you hanging forever. I allow two months for the agent to respond. If I can't get an answer, or the answer is no, I begin the process over again with another skater and agent. In many instances, I am still dealing with contracts and agents right up to the last minute.

And then there are the skaters who are booked far in advance, but are forced to pull out because of an injury or a dire personal reason. Just when I think I have finished dealing with the negotiators of our business, I have to pick up the phone and begin the process again.

While I am navigating this shark-infested water, Lou-Anne is booking the venue, attempting to get sponsors on board, and arranging for the hotel, catering, and transportation. Once we have a fair idea of who is going to be appearing in the show, Isabelle begins the arduous task of finding out what music the skaters are planning to perform to so she can supply the information to the television network.

Isabelle

Because Dreams on Ice is usually taped for future television viewing, one of my major responsibilities is supplying the network with the titles of the music the skaters will be performing to. This is necessary because the network must clear the music through the original artists and producers. If a show is to be aired within a twenty-four-hour period, the clearing isn't necessary, but because Dreams on Ice is considered an exhibition (competitions are also excluded from the necessity of clearing rights) and is shown on television months later, we must go through this process. It becomes even more complicated.

In order for the network to air a piece of music, they have to clear it through two different systems. One is the synchronization rights, which belong to the producer who originally put the music together. The other is the master tracks, which are owned by the artist who first performed the song. If one or the other of these rights is not granted, and the skater still wants to use the music, there are only a few options left. We can arrange to have the same piece of music redone by different artists or musicians, which can be costly and time-consuming, and often we don't find out until just before show time that a certain piece won't clear. Outside of performing an entirely different number, the only other consideration is to use the music that won't clear, knowing that when the number airs, the network will have selected a variation of the original piece, or another song altogether, which may not match up with the skater's performance. The skater also stands the chance that his or her number may be deleted from the final tape, and it will be as if that performer hadn't been on the show at all.

When I submit my list of titles to the network, they in turn contact all the necessary people, who can charge anywhere from 500 to 10,000 dollars per piece to release the rights for one performance. When you are looking at clearing twenty pieces of music, the total cost can be exorbitant. The networks absorb the expense, but depending on the revenue created by the show, they may not want to spend a great deal of money on one piece.

I prefer to get the music from the skaters two months in advance. The earlier I submit the titles to the network, the sooner we will find out if they have been cleared. However, I do have a very difficult time approaching skaters in the summer about what music they will be performing to in the fall. Lloyd and I rarely know what we will be skating to that early. In the past, we sometimes left it too late. Then when we selected numbers with music that had already been cleared for previous performances, we just assumed the music would clear again. We soon discovered that is not always the case.

Lloyd

In 1998, we skated to a Bette Midler song that had cleared earlier for a Stars on Ice televised performance. When we decided to skate to it at our show the following September, we couldn't get the number cleared. We skated to it anyway. When it aired months later, the viewers didn't see Isabelle and I skating to a Bette Midler tune. Although it was the same song, it was performed by a different artist and musicians.

How music can clear for one performance and not the next, no one really understands. Perhaps the producer or artist wants too much money from the network, or maybe they have a limit on how many times an individual act can use their music. Sometimes I think the decision is made arbitrarily, that it depends on nothing more simple than the mood of the person taking the request. Whatever the case, some skaters become very annoyed when we tell them that their music didn't clear. Because most skaters aren't involved in the production end of a show, they don't realize that a producer must submit a request for each performance. They make the mistake of thinking, like Isabelle and I did, that because the piece cleared for show A, it will automatically clear for show B.

If skaters can't get their music cleared and choose to perform the number anyway, they must be prepared for the consequences. In 1997, Isabelle and I skated to "I'll Be There for You," by the Rembrandts, but were unable to obtain clearance for Dreams on Ice. When the network aired the show, we were both taken aback by the music they chose to accompany our performance. Although it was a lively piece and similar in tempo, there were no vocals and it was something that neither of us would have elected to skate to. Unnoticeable to most people, but obvious to Isabelle and me, were the couple of skating elements that didn't match up to the music at all.

Even worse was something that occurred during our debut show. We had unveiled a new number by Barbra Streisand, entitled, "Somewhere." People who saw it live commented that it was one of our most beautiful performances, but because the music wouldn't clear then or ever, "Somewhere" was never seen by a television audience.

Isabelle

The year after my father died, I heard an Eric Clapton piece that I wanted to skate to. "Tears in Heaven" was a very moving song, written by the artist after the death of his young son. Because of my dad's recent passing, I felt connected to the lyrics and thought skating to the piece would be a wonderful tribute to my father. When the music didn't clear, I contacted Eric Clapton's agent in England. I wrote a letter explaining my feelings, and hoped that my request might somehow be passed on to his client. Soon after, we received clearance from Eric Clapton to use his music for that one performance. I was so thankful, because I realized that this song was very personal to him, and that he didn't want it exploited in any way. Although Lloyd and I skated to "Tears in Heaven" for a couple of competitions, Dreams on Ice was the only exhibition event that saw it televised.

Because of the many problems associated with clearing music, some skaters have music composed for them. Torvill and Dean take this approach, as do Kurt Browning and Brian Boitano. Kurt performs to a number that the rock group Tragically Hip wrote for him, and Brian skates to pieces composed by a friend of his who is appearing in *The Phantom of the Opera*.

Lloyd and I have the music written for the opening and closing themes of Dreams on Ice, which assures us that these important segments will be aired. Karl Hugo, a pianist from Montreal, first began composing for us in 1994. For that performance, Karl played the music on a plexiglas grand piano that sat on a corner of the ice. The audience and skaters loved it, and since then, Karl has written all the overtures and finales for Dreams on Ice. He is an amazing musician who understands what works best on the ice, and has even composed individual numbers for the Duchesnays and Bourne and Kraatz. By 1997, Karl was so popular that he released a CD entitled "Freestyle," which showcased his original themes for Dreams on Ice.

Lloyd

After months of planning, Isabelle and I usually arrive in Windsor a few days before the show, which is always scheduled for a Saturday night. Having everything in place before the skaters' arrival is of the utmost importance. I want them to feel comfortable and catered to, and we do everything to ensure this. Along with Lou-Anne and Isabelle, I check on the hotel preparations, the transportation to and from the rink, which is usually supplied by volunteers, and the menus for the various functions we host during the weekend. We also liaise with sports photographer Marc Evon, who will provide us with photos for future publicity and programs. Marc, one of the best in the business, has been doing much of our photography for years.

It is our custom to give gifts to the skaters, such as tracksuits and warm-up jackets, which are donated by various sponsors. I negotiate for these items over a number of months, so when I get to Windsor, I make sure they have been delivered to the hotel. After meeting with everyone, I head to the arena to check on preparations there. The condition of the ice surface, dressing rooms, seating, and advertising on the rink boards are my responsibility. And once we begin the setup and rehearsals, I oversee the lighting, music, and dealing with the television crew. Someone has to be the heavy, and because I am the most outspoken of the three personalities producing the show, these duties tend to fall on my shoulders. If something is wrong, it needs to be taken care of immediately and I have no problem in demanding perfection.

Isabelle, who is more tactful than I am, looks after the skaters. She sees to their needs and generally tries to keep them happy. Although the majority of skaters we invite are fairly easy to work with, there is the odd one who can be demanding. Isabelle deals with difficult situations calmly, whereas I don't always have the patience.

Isabelle

We have been doing Dreams on Ice for so long now, that as soon as we arrive in Windsor, Lloyd and I go about our business in a very routine manner. Knowing what has to be done, we immediately set about on our individual tasks.

First I meet with Lou-Anne to see if there are any loose ends that need tying up with respect to the hotel arrangements. Then I concentrate on looking after the skaters. Before they arrive, I put itineraries and gifts in their rooms. With so many functions for the skaters to attend, knowing ahead of time where they have to be, and when, puts them more at ease. Lloyd and I know how we like to be treated when we are at events and we attempt to show our guests the same consideration.

Sometimes Lloyd and I are scheduled to make publicity appearances that might generate more ticket sales. We usually try to schedule these on the days before the skaters arrive, on Friday morning. Between Lou-Anne and I, and local volunteers, we make sure they are picked up at the airport and brought to the hotel.

Early Friday will find Lloyd at the rink, organizing practices and rehearsals. When I join him later that morning, I have my own checklist to attend to. Is there coffee in the dressing rooms? Are there towels in the showers? Do we have a steamer for the costumes? Do we have a person on-site to mend an outfit that might get ripped during rehearsals? Is the food set up for lunch? All the skaters come to me with their questions and I have to be prepared to answer them.

On Friday afternoon, we hold a press reception at the hotel for the media. All the skaters are asked to attend, as the event is usually reported in the evening papers or news broadcasts, and may again lead to last-minute ticket sales.

In the early evening, we open the rink to the public, and fans can skate side by side with their favorite athletes who are appearing in the show. This event usually attracts more than two hundred people and the skaters spend much of their time signing autographs. One year, Jozef Sabovcik brought his son, Blade, to the open skate. The four-year-old was quickly surrounded by autograph seekers. Blade had just learned to print and although he couldn't quite master writing all the letters to his name on one page, he patiently scribbled in each autograph book, and was very charming to the crowd of little girls who wanted to be near him.

Later, our company, BBE, hosts a buffet dinner for the skaters, friends, and other people involved in the production of the show. It's a time for everyone to relax a little and take a deep breath. Usually we go to bed early that night, because there won't be any rest until hours after Dreams on Ice has finished. Once the show is over, there is yet another reception to thank our sponsors and guests. And then there is the inevitable party, which is an informal gathering of the skaters and close friends, and which often doesn't end until two or three in the morning. Other than stopping by to say goodnight, I usually let the others do the partying for me. I'm just too tired after the show.

The day of the production sees Lloyd and me at the rink very early. Although we don't have to worry about choreographing the production, we are in charge of the rehearsals. Lloyd created the choreography the first year, and although he did a great job, there were just too many other things for him to worry about. The following year we decided to produce the show in a more professional manner and hired choreographer Lea Ann Miller, who is renowned in the business, and worked with us for many years.

Lloyd

We try to move through the rehearsals quickly and not leave people standing around for too long. The rink is cold and the skaters can get edgy if they believe their time is being wasted. However, when television is involved, maintaining a fast pace is not always possible. So I attempt to compromise. The television crew may inform me they require two hours for some setup, and I will give them only one. I hate lengthy rehearsals, and we have too much to cover in one day as it is.

As hard as we all work at the rehearsals, we also have lots of fun. I can recall one instance in particular that still brings a smile to my face when I think about it. We were in the middle of rehearsals, where Barb Underhill and Paul Martini were skating to "When a Man Loves a Woman." Barb was over Paul's head in a lift and was just beginning the dismount. At the exact moment in the music when the vocals sing out, "She can bring you down," Barb descended and caught her hand in Paul's plastic track pants, which came down around his ankles. Because Barb couldn't get untangled, the pair skaters were caught in a position unlike anything I have ever seen. She was wrapped around his bare legs, while the two of them kept sliding down the ice until they hit the flowers at the other end of the rink. Barb was laughing hysterically the whole time, and of course, we all joined in. Although Paul was a good sport about it later, I am not sure if he thought it was as funny as we did when it happened. But what a sight they made. If the mishap had been a planned and judged comedic routine, there is no doubt in my mind it would have received perfect tens.

Isabelle

A couple of years ago, Lou-Anne and I coordinated a fashion show in conjunction with Dreams on Ice. Most of the skaters we invited that weekend participated in the show, including Lloyd and myself. Although I was a little nervous, I found that once I was on the runway, I relaxed immediately and enjoyed modeling the clothes. Perhaps I am so used to performing in front of an audience, that it doesn't matter if I am on skates or in high-heels (though I was a little afraid of falling off my shoes!). I believe the other skaters felt the same way, as most of them appeared to be naturals. For instance, because of a flight delay, Brian Orser arrived at the show just an hour before it began. Because he was so late, he hadn't been able to take part in any of the rehearsals, but as soon as Brian stepped on the runway, you would have thought he had been modeling all his life. He was that good.

One of the best segments in the show featured leatherwear, and onstage were two powerful-looking motorcycles. Stephen Cousins, Denis Petrov, Jozef Sabovcik, Rocky Marval, Brian Orser, and Lloyd came out wearing leather chaps, jackets, vests, and pants. They looked so macho and tough, you would have thought they were part of a motorcycle gang rather than figure skaters. And when Lloyd sat on one of the Harley-Davidsons (his favorite mode of transportation, by the way), I knew my partner felt right at home.

Lloyd

Isabelle and I have done much of the commentating for Dreams on Ice. We don't review the individual skaters, but we are taped through a series of interviews to announce aspects of the show.

Although Isabelle had the opportunity to commentate once before at the 1994 World Championships, she told me she wasn't comfortable. My partner was doing it solo, and believed that's why she was unable to relax. I know how she feels because we seem to work better as a team, and I also prefer to have her at my side.

We have been together so long and have probably given hundreds of television interviews. When we are speaking to reporters, they may as well be speaking to one person, as Isabelle and I often finish each other's sentences. We just know one another that well. There is also a natural chemistry between the two of us that somehow makes for a good interview.

What the audience doesn't see is the two of us before the interview. In an attempt to get our thoughts organized, we will discuss what we want to bring up with the reporter. Usually we are glad that we have taken the time for this ritual. I tend to be very frank, especially if I am upset about a particular issue, and Isabelle will often veto a remark that I was planning to make. Respecting her opinion, and not wanting to upset her, I generally comply.

During the interview, Isabelle and I will silently signal each other. If I think a question should be answered by my partner, I will pull on the back of her sleeve and vice versa. We also give each other gentle nudges, if one of us is talking too long.

Commentating for television is something I would definitely like to pursue in the future. If I can't be on the ice skating, sitting at the rink's edge and describing what I see would probably be the next best thing.

Isabelle

When I tried commentating for a French network a few years ago, I found it very difficult. It's ironic, because I used to think that I would like to go into that line of work someday. I even studied communications in college. But after my stint as a commentator at the 1994 Worlds, I turned off the idea.

Since then, Lloyd and I have done some television announcing for Dreams on Ice, which I found enjoyable. Although I still don't want to commentate on a full-time basis, I liked talking to the audience with Lloyd. It was much the same as when we give interviews. The two of us fit like an old glove and can often read each other's thoughts. We also trust one another, and know that neither of us would let the other say something that might sound foolish or uncalled for. Every now and then, however, certain comments slip out. If Lloyd is in a temper, no amount of nudging from me is going to curtail his sharp words to the press. A few times, I have even kicked him under the table—with my skate on! Even that won't stop him if he is off on a tangent. But television commentating for Dreams on Ice is an entirely different thing. The setting is relaxed and we are speaking about something that we know and care about.

Lloyd

If the audience were to come backstage an hour before the show, they would see chaos. This isn't unique to Dreams on Ice. Every skating show is the same, because no matter how much planning has gone into the event, something always goes awry: skaters are getting into their costumes, when suddenly an outfit tears; someone else's costume wasn't steamed properly; a skate lace breaks.

During this hour, Isabelle, Lou-Anne, and I frantically run around backstage, trying to look after everyone. Meanwhile, Lou-Anne is also worrying about the sponsors being happy, the presentation of the check to the foundation that occurs at halftime, and her emceeing at the start of the show, which is intended to warm up the audience. Isabelle and I are also thinking about our own numbers and the opening and closing segments. On all our minds are the television cameras. When the crew tells us they are ready to go, we must be in our places. Once the taping begins, each portion of the production is timed and we adhere to a strict schedule.

However, when the show actually starts is quite another matter. The programs indicate a seven-thirty opening, but television is notorious for running late. They tell us to be ready in fifteen minutes, and then make us wait for another ten. There is nothing worse than getting dressed, putting your skates on, then having to sit there. The skaters are nervous backstage, as it is. Geared up to step on the ice, we want to go.

Throughout all the activity backstage, the one constant voice is that of the floor manager, who begins to call out the time a half hour before the show, and continues the countdown to show time. At this point, some skaters are warming up and others are going over the steps for the group opening number. When the floor manager yells out, "Five minutes," I feel a familiar rush of adrenaline. Everything has been done to the best of our ability and now I must concentrate on skating well. He signals us to take our places. We stand at the curtain that separates us from the audience, which has been clapping and cheering for the last few minutes. The last word we hear from the floor manager is "Ready," and finally we are on the ice.

One year, the unthinkable happened. The Windsor arena is very old but is the only venue in the city that can accommodate a large audience. On the night of the show, Windsor was hit with torrential rains, and the roof started to leak. As people were walking into the arena, rain was falling on their heads. Several volunteers were cleaning up the water as best they could; others were shifting the audience from one side of the seating area to the other, which left gaping holes in the stands, apparent on camera afterwards. Many audience members had to be placed in chairs right on the ice, because there wasn't enough dry seating to accommodate everyone. I was trying to deal with matters backstage, and also running out to check on the stands and the ice surface every few minutes. It was a very stressful night.

Isabelle

I thought most of the skaters took the leaking roof in stride. Kurt Browning performed to "Singing in the Rain," and in the middle of his number, playfully splashed in some water that had pooled on the ice. He even borrowed an umbrella from a woman in the audience. The most comical sight was the spotlight operators, positioned at the roof level. They continued doing their jobs as if they hadn't a care in the world, each holding an umbrella to keep the rain off their heads and equipment.

I know Lloyd was upset with this mishap. He was worried about how it would look on television. He is also always the stickler for a perfect ice surface. His greatest concern was for the skaters and their safety. On that night, though, there wasn't much any of us could do. It was too late to cancel the show, so we just reseated as many of the audience as possible and made the best of a bad situation.

Lloyd

In 1998, Dreams on Ice wasn't televised for the first time in seven years. BBS, the network we were under contract with, had been bought out by CTV, and because of some major restructuring, our show fell through the cracks. Despite its award-winning standing and uniqueness in Canada, our contract wasn't renewed. Currently, we are negotiating with another network to broadcast the 1999 show. I certainly hope this occurs, as, without television, we stand to lose much of our already limited budget.

No matter what happens, I hope Dreams on Ice will continue. The show has become a passion for me, and even without the benefit of television revenues, I believe we could make it work with some sacrifices and adaptations. After learning that Dreams on Ice wasn't going to be picked up for television, we presented two concurrent shows in September. One was in Oshawa, and the other in Windsor the following night. Although we had been worried about finances, we managed to break even and have some money left over to give to the foundation.

Moreover, we have already presented two shows in London and one in Brampton, which we called Winter Dreams on Ice. These events were not planned for television, but they proved to be popular where they were staged. Through them we were able to raise more money for the Children's Wish Foundation. In total, Dreams on Ice has donated more than two hundred and fifty thousand dollars to the foundation. If it is up to me, Isabelle and I will continue doing whatever it takes to help the children.

Isabelle

It didn't bother me that Dreams on Ice wasn't televised in 1998. The show was actually easier to do without television involved. However, I am not the one who is worrying about the budget. I also wouldn't keep the show going if we were to start losing thousands of dollars, because we still have to pay the skaters, the crew, and other expenses. If we are unable to meet our goal of making money for the children, it would seem futile to continue with the show. I sincerely hope it doesn't come to that. Though we love doing Dreams on Ice, we also have to be realistic.

Lloyd

I would like to think that Dreams on Ice will continue to be viable long after Isabelle and I retire from skating. Currently, the team of Brasseur and Eisler are a drawing feature, but Canadian athletes such as Emanuel Sandhu, Elvis Stojko, Shae-Lynn Bourne and Victor Kraatz are also huge calling cards to an audience. If, and when, these skaters turn professional, any one of them could pick up the reins and carry on the tradition of Dreams on Ice.

But even if I am not skating in the show, I would like to continue to produce it with Isabelle. If she walked away, I don't think I would do it without her. It isn't that I expect my career after skating to revolve around Isabelle. When our time together on the ice ends, we will likely pursue different ventures. Our individual goals have changed over the last few years, and we don't share the same ideas about our future, as a team or separately. But we undertook Dreams on Ice together and I wouldn't want to do it without Isabelle being involved.

Isabelle

I don't know what will happen to Dreams on Ice when Lloyd and I quit skating. Although I feel fortunate to be able to skate for a living now, I am growing tired of the daily grind. Sometimes I am so burnt out that I have trouble deciding what I want to do tomorrow, let alone five years from now. I do know that I would like to go on helping the Children's Wish Foundation in some way.

I am sure that it must be frustrating to Lloyd that I don't have the same ambition and drive that he does. He wants to accomplish so much in life but I just don't have the fire anymore. For years we shared the same goals, and we thought that the team of Brasseur and Eisler would go on forever in one way or another. When we were amateur skaters, we worked together to skate our best at the Olympics and World Championships. After turning professional, our ambition was united in our desire to become better entertainers. Now things have changed. I eventually want to lead a quieter, simpler life, and I don't think that matches up with Lloyd's plans. It must disappoint him and sometimes I feel guilty, but I have to be happy too.

CHAPTER THREE

Competing

Lloyd

OCCASIONALLY I still feel animosity when I think about how our chance at winning an Olympic gold medal was taken away from us. Because of a rule change, professional skaters were allowed to participate in the most important competition of our lives. Without them, the 1994 gold medal would have belonged to us. Instead, Isabelle and I had to settle for bronze.

Both the Russian pairs that reinstated had already won gold at previous Olympics. Gordeeva and Grinkov claimed the 1988 Olympic title, while Mishkutenok and Dmitriev were the best in 1992. In both cases, the top *amateur* skaters won the coveted prize. Isabelle and I, however, weren't given that opportunity. When we became the best in the amateur world in 1993, it was a given that if we kept at the top of our game, the Olympic gold would be ours in 1994. It never crossed our minds that in a competition that has been amateur associated since its conception, paid professionals would be allowed to re-enter the field. Of course they would beat us. Both teams had sufficient time to polish their artistic and entertainment skills on the professional circuit, but hadn't been away from the amateur world long enough to have compromised their technical ability. As it turned out, Gordeeva and Grinkov placed first, and Mishkutenok and Dmitriev came second. What it proved was something Isabelle and I already knew. We were the best of the amateurs.

In 1998, Ottavio Cinquanta, president of the International Skating Union (ISU), declared that professional figure skaters would never again be considered eligible for the Olympics. In his words, inviting them back in 1994 didn't work out. It was just too bad the ISU had to test the waters when it was our turn. Isabelle and I had worked for years towards that one goal and were finally at our peak in 1994. It was *our* time, as it had been the Russian pair skaters' time before us. But with an ill-planned and hasty decision, the ISU drastically altered the course of our lives.

An Olympic gold medal means everything in this business. Not winning the gold meant the loss of a tremendous amount of money. Lucrative endorsements disappeared, and appearance fees dropped to at least a third of what they would have been had we placed first. Although money is not my motivation for skating, I would have to be a fool not to care how those funds could have secured our futures. What irks me the most, however, is that we will never be considered in the same league as Olympic champions. There will be no asterisk beside our names in the record books, explaining the circumstances surrounding the 1994 games. Although we will be remembered for many accomplishments, winning that gold medal will not be one of them. To be an Olympic champion merits respect. It was an honor that was rightfully ours, and one we will never know.

Isabelle

As I said earlier, I used to believe that once we became professional skaters, the politics that were associated with competing would disappear. However, they were only to take on a different guise. In professional skating, ticket sales and television ratings are the bottom line. Actual competitions appear to become secondary, and the ethics of staging them often fall by the wayside.

Prize money is given out at the competitions that Lloyd and I are invited to. In most cases, the amount we receive varies according to many factors, and not just on how well we will skate. In the pairs division, there are usually three or four teams competing, guaranteed a certain sum of money before they even step on the ice. In the beginning, I assumed that we were all promised the same amount, but during our first year of competing as pros, I heard that the guarantees varied depending on the circumstances and the skaters involved.

The problem I saw was that if the team that had been guaranteed a lower amount skated better than the rest of us and won the event, the organizer would have to pay them more money, plus they would have to pay the other two teams the higher amounts of money they had been promised. Hence, in almost every competition in which we have participated, the skaters place in the order of the original guarantee. Because this has happened so many times, it seems obvious to me that the organizers of the competitions must approach the judges beforehand and request the order they want to see us finish in. I don't think all judges go along with this tactic. However, it is unlikely that those who don't comply will be invited back to judge the following year's competition.

When I discovered what was happening behind the scenes, I wondered why these events were even called competitions. Throughout our amateur career, we had to cope with judges sometimes favoring competitors from their own countries, and rumors and innuendoes of supposed deal-making. But what I was now seeing in professional competition was unbelievable to me. I found it especially upsetting that there were spectators in the stands and at home who believed these events were true competitions instead of the shows that they actually were.

Considering our personalities, you would think this would have bothered Lloyd more than me. But in reality, I had a harder time than Lloyd dealing with the pretense. Lloyd's attitude was far more laid back. He would say to me, "Let's go out there and put on a good show." Because we placed first a few times when we were guaranteed otherwise, I think Lloyd preferred to believe the competitions were judged fairly. However, I rarely see anyone who is guaranteed fourth place actually win an event, or even come second.

Lloyd

It became clear to me early on that winning a professional competition isn't always based on how well a person skates. I believe it has more to do with who has an Olympic gold medal, and what country they are from, than guarantees.

In our first season as professionals, the judging was still as politically biased as ever. In pairs, Russian skaters automatically receive a two-point advantage over North Americans. Because they have dominated the pairs discipline for decades, everyone assumes they are going to be the best team on the ice. Professional competitions appeared to be no different than amateur competition. Therefore, I decided from the beginning to concentrate only on going out and skating well. Whether we were going to get credit for a great performance eventually became irrelevant. I am not saying that placing second, when we should have been first, has never disturbed me. It very often did. But I learned to feel satisfied if I knew that Isabelle and I had outskated our competitors, regardless of the final results.

Unlike Isabelle, however, when we enter a professional competition with guarantees, I would still like to believe that we have a chance to win. I go into each competition with the same attitude: I want to have prepared an outstanding number, then skate to our highest ability for the audience. Although I usually have an idea how we may place, I would rather give the judges something to mark. If we do, there is always the hope that we may do better.

I don't think the guarantee system is unfair. It entices skaters to participate in an event, and then, depending on how we place, we may be able to earn even more money on top of the guarantee. That's just the nature of professional skating—you are paid a fee to skate, while the promoters are trying to run a competition around the event. It is no different than paying track athletes to show up and compete in a race. The most important thing is to put on a good show for the audience and maintain some optimism that the judges will appreciate our efforts.

What I do believe is unfair is that pairs skaters are paid much less than singles skaters. A first-place win at a competition rewards skaters with decent prize money, but the pairs have to split the win, while a singles skater receives the entire amount. In my opinion, we work twice as hard for half the money. For years I have been lobbying to pay the pairs and dancers at least a third more; so far my voice has had no effect. Only in the eligible world, where the rules were recently changed to allow skaters to earn prize money for winning international events, has there been an increase in the money for couples. An eligible singles skater who wins the World Championships currently receives fifty thousand dollars, while the winning pairs and dancers earn seventy-five thousand, which is then split between them.

Isabelle

Even though I usually know where Lloyd and I will end up in a competition, we still try to skate our best. Because of all the years I spent training as a competitive athlete, something comes over me before I step on the ice. And the feeling fires me up. I still want us to excel and be admired for what we do. For the few minutes we are on the ice, I actually forget where I am and what the competition is all about. It is just me and my partner, striving to perform well. Only when we get off the ice and see the results does the reality of the situation come back to me.

Moreover, I still get as nervous before a competition as I did in my amateur days. During that time in our careers, Lloyd and I trained hard and skated well to get to the podium at the Worlds. We don't have that goal anymore, but we still want to be proud of ourselves. Therefore, landing the throws and jumps means just as much to me. I don't want people to leave after a competition saying, "Brasseur and Eisler can't do anything anymore. Why don't they retire?"

As much as I desire to perform at a high level at professional competitions, the titles mean absolutely nothing to me. In fact, if I had a choice between winning or a standing ovation, I would definitely pick the standing ovation. Later in life, I know I will never get a sense of achievement just from coming first at any of the professional competitions Lloyd and I entered. When I look back over our time as professionals, all I want to be remembered for is how much people enjoyed watching us perform.

Lloyd

Isabelle and I take every professional competition we enter very seriously. The two of us are extremely competitive. Even though we would still be paid, regardless of our performance, we would not go into a competition unprepared. Letting down our fans in that way goes against who we are. The quality of our skating, the choreography of the numbers, our technical skill, and costumes must all be up to our customary high standard. If we are not satisfied with any one of those aspects, we would rather not participate in an event. Isabelle and I have too much pride, and have worked too long, to jeopardize our reputations.

In this age of being paid big bucks just to show up at a competition, we sometimes see skaters who are overweight, undertrained, and generally not ready to compete. Once Olympic or World champions, they may be striving to make a comeback, and that can be sad to witness. Others just don't take skating seriously enough, and it is my conviction, some are participating in competitions out of greed. Many of these skaters should take a second look at themselves and realize what an embarrassment they are to the sport. They are invited to the current competitions because of what they once accomplished. An Olympic champion sells tickets. Even though they may be skating like a novice, they will always be asked to enter a competition. Unfortunately, how they skate at these events is also how they will be remembered.

I never want to skate and have people say, "Brasseur and Eisler should really give it up. They are just not what they used to be." I would much rather our fans wonder why Isabelle and I quit while we were still at the top. I want to be remembered as a World champion, not as a has-been.

Appearing even at one competition when we aren't up to par is unthinkable. In 1997, we were supposed to compete at the World Team Championship, which was one of the first competitions of the season for us. Because Isabelle was married and residing in the United States, and I was living in Canada, we were having trouble getting together to train. After finding a suitable center that was near Isabelle's home, we began to rehearse intensively, but the practices weren't going well. Our level of skating was probably no higher than twenty percent of the hundred percent at which it should have been, and two weeks before the competition, we were ready to pull out.

Desperate for help, we called our coach, Josée Picard, in Montreal and asked her to work with us. Josée agreed to fly in, and within three days Isabelle and I were back to skating respectably. We weren't perfect, but by drawing on past performances, we knew we would be able to compete. However, if Josée had been unavailable, and we had not been able to achieve the excellence we always aim for, Isabelle and I would have refused to go to the competition. As it turned out, not only did we skate well at the World Team Championship, there were also many comments about what good shape we were in, considering how early it was in the season.

Isabelle

In July or August, Lloyd and I sit down and review our invitations to compete that season. We look at the routines we have already prepared for the previous winter and spring tours to decide if any of them would be appropriate for competition. We also determine if any past competitive programs would be suitable. If, for example, we had competed with a number only once the previous season, we might decide to use it for a different competition in the fall. When we know what we can take from our repertoire, then we begin to plan how many new competitive numbers will be required for the upcoming competitions. This can result in quite a few, because certain competitions, such as the World Team and the World Challenge, are run by the same television network. Since the competitions may be airing within a few weeks of each other, they don't want the same numbers repeated.

In this regard, professional competitions are far more difficult to organize and train for than amateur competitions. The eligible skaters have only two programs they must practice, and they compete with these same programs all season. As professionals, between September and December alone, we sometimes have to rehearse and train as many as ten individual programs. Although some of those numbers are meant to be performed in shows, they still have to be practiced the same way. A few times, we tried to revamp some of our show numbers into competitive programs, but we discovered that cutting corners can take away from the overall effect. The number remains the same, but the elements in it change, and aren't always consistent with our original concept for the program. Although it can be time-consuming to develop, a number should be created for a specific purpose, whether that be strictly for entertainment, or for competition, which will be a combination of both technical skills and artistry.

Lloyd

By August, we know what our lineup of competitions will be for the next skating season. It is then that we begin to discuss ideas and crack out some new competitive programs. By that time, we normally have our exhibition numbers in place for the artistic side of our upcoming appearances. Some of those would have been created in the spring for the Stars on Ice and Tom Collins tours, and may be ones we can adapt for the artistic portion of a competition.

Preparing for professional competition is very complex because we have to include technical elements that judges will be able to decipher. The judges will usually want to see the typical side-by-side jumps and at least one throw in the technical half of a competition. But Isabelle and I like to perform the many elements that we have invented, such as the chainsaw, fly high–say bye, and the triple lateral twist. Because no one else performs these moves, the judges often have no idea of their difficulty.

The artistic segments of the competition cause us just as many headaches. Many people in the skating world believe that in order to be artistic, you must be balletic. They want to see slow numbers skated to Mozart or Beethoven. To Isabelle and me, however, artistic means being creative, and interpreting whatever music we have selected to skate to in the best fashion possible. Our "Blues Brothers," "The Disco," and "Lady and the Man" numbers are all fast, upbeat, and fun, and we consider them all highly artistic. Moreover, they each contain extremely difficult elements. But because the moves are considered adagio or acrobatic, and are not in the rule book, we can be marked down by a panel of judges who, more often than not, prefer flowing costumes, classical music, and traditional skating.

Since we want to ensure that our skating will be entertaining as well as technically sound, it takes considerable thought and planning to combine the two in a program the judges will value. If we went out and skated at a competition strictly to entertain, we might come first in the audience's opinion, but we could also count on being dead last with the judges.

At the 1994 World Professional Skating Championships, we performed our "Lady and the Man" number for the artistic part of the competition. We were sitting in second place after the technical segment and had a good chance of winning. Although this variation of our routine was relatively new, everyone who had seen Isabelle and I perform the number in recent weeks was in total awe. In fact, we made the front page of several major newspapers when it was debuted, and were applauded for the unique style. When we finished the competition, we received a standing ovation from the Landover, Maryland, crowd. But the judges marked us third. The other skaters had performed slow numbers, and because our program wasn't what the judges were used to seeing, we got crushed. I don't believe the judges understood the program's artistry. I also don't think they could accept that a program in which a man dresses up like a woman, could possibly come first. Rather, they probably thought it would give skating a bad name.

My response to this particular set of judges was also something they didn't see too often. I flipped my arm to them. Isabelle told me afterwards that I shouldn't react in this manner. But at least I was honest. The judging wasn't the only reason I was upset at that particular competition. I was fed up with being shot down for trying to bring something different to skating. We put much work and thought into a program that was packed with technical ability and, in many respects, was more difficult to execute than the other competitors' numbers. I also couldn't fathom how an audience of fifteen thousand could love a program, and at the same time how a panel of nine judges could hate it.

However, you live and you learn. Our experience was not going to stop us from being innovative and performing the type of numbers we prefer. But Isabelle and I realized that if we wanted to be taken seriously, we would have to bend a little now and then. Therefore, when we now plan a competitive program, we consider every aspect of the competition in which it will be performed.

We also have to train extensively for competitions, and in my experience, it is far more difficult than the training we had to do in the eligible ranks. Because we are practicing numerous programs at the same time, it would be impossible to do this in our two daily sessions of one and a half hours. I leave it up to Isabelle to plan out the schedule, who will organize what we are rehearsing on any given day.

Isabelle

If we didn't have a schedule to keep us organized, we could never hope to be ready for the season. There are just too many numbers to practice. In this area, I try to keep us on track. I figure out how much time we will need for each number and how many days we will spend practicing it. Usually, we concentrate on three numbers each day. Any more would be too much.

There is much technical training involved in our competitive numbers, and Josée helps us with that from September to December. Before we work with her, we usually get together with a choreographer, who helps us to create the program. Although Lloyd and I most often select the music and have an idea of the routine we want, it is the choreographer who will polish and refine it. Over the years we have worked with several choreographers, such as Lea Ann Miller, Jean-Pierre Boulais, and Julie Marcotte. More recently, we have gone back to Uschi Keszler, who helped to create many of our amateur programs. We vary the choreographers we use, because if we worked with one person on a continual basis, our style would always look the same, and performing different types of numbers has become our trademark. We never get bored, and as a result the audience maintains its interest in us as a team.

Lloyd

Until 1996, and with the exception of our first year in professional skating, when neither of us knew what to expect, our training for competitions had always been intense and structured. Isabelle and I both lived in Quebec and trained at the same rink in Boucherville. That all changed, however, when Isabelle married American pairs champion Rocky Marval, and moved across the border.

    Their wedding took place in August 1996, and understandably, Isabelle had little time for training that summer. Neither of us was too concerned, because we were booked for only two competitions that season—the Canadian Pro and the Ultimate Four, a pro/am competition that we had won previously. The cutback that year was a result of a deletion of the pairs segment in two competitions that we usually participated in. Fox Rock and Roll, which we had also won the year before, decided to concentrate on singles skating only, and the World Team competition was alternating between pairs and dance teams, along with the singles skaters. Although we had been invited to the World Professional Skating Championships, our first experience at that competition had been so bad that I wasn't yet ready to return.

    Over the season, we heard from many fans who told us they missed seeing us at the competitions, and by the summer of 1997 we decided to enter as many events as possible that autumn. By following this course, we realized that we would have to get ourselves organized ahead of time. Isabelle was now firmly settled in New Jersey and I was still living in Boucherville, Quebec. Where would we train?

We had various options. Isabelle could have come to Boucherville, and although we did train there for a few weeks, she was a newlywed and wanted to be at home with her husband as much as possible. We could have both gone to Simsbury, Connecticut, where there is a training center we have often used in the past. However, it is located about three hours from Isabelle's residence, and although the ice was available, we didn't see the sense in both of us leaving home to train somewhere else. After some shopping around, we learned that Uschi Keszler was opening a rink just outside Philadelphia that was within commuting distance of Isabelle's home. The center was supposed to be up and running by the beginning of October, and we made arrangements to train there. When we arrived, however, the rink wasn't ready, which left us in a terrible bind. We immediately began searching for other ice in the area, but learned it was next to impossible to find an arena that would devote sessions just to pair skaters. Instead, the ice was open to anyone who wanted to skate on it.

Because Rocky wanted to see Isabelle while she was at home, he asked us to train with him and his partner, Calla Urbanski, who were doing their practicing on these open-ice sessions. With much reluctance on my part, we ended up training with them on a rink, where some days, there were adults and children who were just learning how to skate, and young competitors practicing for sectionals. Attempting to maneuver around these skaters, and often at high speeds, were Calla, Rocky, Isabelle, and me. It was dangerous. Because we didn't want to get hurt or harm anyone else, it was difficult to concentrate on skating. Isabelle and I had never trained like that. Throughout our entire careers, we have only had pairs on the ice while we practice. I didn't like it and more than once, I lost my temper.

Adding fuel to the fire was that suddenly we were planning our schedules around Rocky and Calla's. In a further attempt to give

Rocky and Isabelle more time together, we agreed to continue training with her husband and his partner as much as we could. Therefore, once Uschi's rink opened, we all began training there. It is a very good facility with double ice and is up to the standards we are accustomed to. But things quickly got out of hand. Now we were attempting to work around four people's schedules, instead of two. It became even more complicated because Calla also coached and had to plan her training time around the classes she taught.

In the past, Isabelle and I had been very organized in our training. We knew what competitions we were going to be participating in and had mapped out our schedule well in advance. Rocky and Calla worked in a different way, and their schedules seemed to be constantly changing. This was no fault of theirs, but I found that it interfered with the way I wanted to train. For example, in an attempt to make things easier for Isabelle and Rocky, the four of us would set aside a week to train together in Philadelphia, when the new rink opened. Because I was the only single person at the time, and didn't have to plan around any significant other, it didn't matter to me when we trained, as long we did it. More important to me was having a sufficient amount of practice time and the right atmosphere to train in. However, I would arrive in Philadelphia, to discover that Rocky and Calla's schedule had been changed, and would be expected to shift our schedule to suit them. The situation became increasingly frustrating to me and resulted in some heated arguments.

In the beginning I was terrified of what was happening. There just didn't seem to be any way to organize us and keep everybody happy. However, with some patience and a few loud discussions, things began to fall into a pattern, and by the end of the autumn, we finally settled into a familiar and comfortable routine.

Isabelle

Trying to adjust to a new lifestyle after I married was something that Lloyd and I had to work on. Of course, Rocky and I wanted to spend time together. We are on the road separately for so much of the year that every spare moment is precious. But as much as I want to spend time with my husband, I realized early on that he and I would have to make sacrifices. Some weeks we will be together and some weeks we won't.

Lloyd and I attempted to plan a schedule with Calla and Rocky's, but it became almost impossible to do. There were just too many people involved. As much as I love my husband and want to be with him, as long as Lloyd and I are skating, I have to do what he and I think is best with respect to our careers. We now lay out our schedule, just as we did before Rocky and I married, and from there I plan with Rocky. But there is no question that sometimes I feel torn between my career and my marriage.

Lloyd

When Isabelle married Rocky, another situation arose that I don't believe any of us had thought about previously. Although Rocky had been my friend for many years, he was also a competitor. Isabelle and I didn't want to skate to any numbers that were like Rocky and Calla's. If we were going to be competing against each other, it was important that our programs be innovative and unique. After a while, though, we began noticing similarities. For instance, one year Isabelle and I had planned on doing a cowboy routine. We had prepared the music and were ready to begin practicing. Then we learned that Calla and Rocky were also working on a country piece.

On hearing that the two teams were intending to compete with numbers that were basically alike, I became very upset. Isabelle was concerned as well. No matter how much we talked with Rocky and Calla, they weren't going to change their program. Isabelle and I were left with only one option. We dumped our routine and came up with "Miss Otis," which became extremely popular with fans and judges alike.

Although I was pleased that our new number fared well, it troubled me that we'd had to give up our original idea. I realized that because Isabelle and Rocky are married to each other, they must obviously talk about skating. Consciously or unconsciously, people were picking up on each other's ideas. And when you have these people competing against each other on the same ice, it doesn't make for an easy time.

Isabelle

One year, both teams came up with a country theme at the same time. I am convinced that it was strictly coincidental. Rocky and Calla, and Lloyd and I are the same style of skaters and we often pick the same type of music and perform many of the same moves. When we learned that Rocky and Calla were planning a number similar to ours, we all looked at each other and said, "Okay, who is going to keep this, and who is going to get rid of it?" Neither team wanted to let their routine go, and for a while, we all dug in our heels. Finally, Lloyd and I backed down, and saved our western number for the following year.

After that incident, I tried telling Rocky ahead of time what Lloyd and I were planning on doing and asked him to make sure that he and Calla didn't come up with the same numbers or moves. However, I don't think Lloyd was crazy about me divulging all our ideas, and I didn't like being caught in the middle. I decided to not talk about skating at all with my husband.

The four of us were appearing in the 1998 Tom Collins Champions on Ice tour and each team had two new numbers to create. Lloyd and I practiced ours in Montreal, and Rocky and Calla prepared theirs in Philadelphia. Rocky and I didn't discuss the programs or the moves. The week before the opening of the tour, the two teams met in Philadelphia to train. Lloyd and I watched Calla and Rocky rehearse and couldn't believe our eyes. They had a move in between their elements that was exactly the same as a new one we had come up with.

Lloyd and I looked at each other in disbelief. In fact, my arms and my mouth opened wide. I just didn't know what to say. When we told Rocky and Calla that their inventive move was included in our program as well, they were also left speechless. There was no way that one team could have known what the other was doing. After that, I decided that the heavy secrecy wasn't worth it. Neither of us is intentionally copying the other's moves, and if a similarity does occur, we will just have to work it out.

When Rocky and I first competed against each other as husband and wife, I had no qualms about going up against him. We have been competing against each other for years, and being married wouldn't affect our performances. When we got together as a couple, it was as Isabelle and Rocky—two people who both happen to skate for a living. Although we are very proud of each other's accomplishments, how we place in the standings has no bearing on our personal relationship. Besides, if we are competing at the same event, the first thing we ask is whether the other has been guaranteed. That way, we both have an idea of the outcome before we even leave home. There are no surprises and no pressure. And although we each have our own performance to concentrate on, being invited to the same competition is actually good news. It means we can spend a few days together, and we are both making money.

During the actual competition, if Rocky goes on before me, I won't watch him skate. I am nervous enough before I get on the ice, and don't like to see anybody else's performance. Rocky understands and respects the way I work. If he skates after me, however, I will most definitely watch him. But I do this as a wife, not as a fellow competitor.

I recall only one instance in which my being married to Rocky could have possibly affected my skating, had the circumstances played out a little differently. In 1997, at the World Challenge, Lloyd and I were competing against two other teams. One of them happened to be Rocky and Calla. Lloyd and I skated first, and after receiving our marks, I lingered by the boards to watch Rocky's performance. They were not long into it when Rocky put Calla up into a lift. Suddenly, a look of pain came over his face, and after lowering Calla, my husband doubled over. The music stopped and Rocky had to be assisted off the ice.

Because I had finished competing, I was able to be by his side immediately and wait with him until he was seen by a doctor, who confirmed that he had injured his back. It was a good thing that Lloyd and I had skated first: I was so worried about Rocky, I am not sure if I could have performed up to par. Hopefully, I would have been professional enough to concentrate on the next five minutes and put him out of my mind. Although I am not certain that would have been possible, I do know that Rocky would never have expected me to cancel or delay my performance because of an injury to him. We are both seasoned professionals, and are very aware that the thousands of people in the audience expect the show to go on.

No matter what happens at a competition, Rocky and I are very supportive of each other. If we skate well, we congratulate each other. If one of us doesn't perform as well as we hoped, we are there for each other to talk to. But we rarely discuss skating at all. Our private time is very precious, so when we are alone, skating is usually the furthest thing from our minds.

Lloyd

Isabelle and I are innovators in our sport as far as the adagio and technical skills of pairs skating go. We invented moves as amateurs and continue to come up with new variations as professionals. Although our desire to be creative is limitless, we are sometimes bound by the reality of what can and can't be done on the ice. Our moves are acrobatic and not usually associated with typical pairs skating. If we look to people in the skating world to help us put new ideas on the ice, we will more often be met with negative comments. People may like our ideas, but don't see how they could possibly be executed on a pair of figure skates. Time and time again, we have proved them wrong.

Sometimes we find our well of creativity drying up. In fact, for two consecutive seasons, we had invented only one new element—the fly high–say bye. Although we never wanted to rest on our laurels, we wondered how much more we could create. Should we listen to the people who were telling us we had done it all? Isabelle and I didn't think so, but we didn't know where to turn for assistance in developing fresh ideas.

During this period I had the opportunity to catch some performances of the celebrated Cirque du Soleil, which was based in Quebec. Their moves and acrobatics were so inventive that I immediately sat up and took notice. If anyone could help Isabelle and I come up with something different, this group could. After discussing it with my partner, we contacted the Cirque du Soleil, and informed them of our plight. They were more than happy to help.

Isabelle

We always try to challenge ourselves, but sometimes we seem to run out of new ideas. There are only so many moves two people can come up with. And personally, I think we have almost reached our limit. So Lloyd and I thought that by working with the Cirque du Soleil, we may learn something different. Their performances are jammed with innovative moves, and when we approached them, they were very cooperative. But when I saw what they wanted me to do, I almost walked out.

The moves they showed us were different, but were far more suitable for a circus performer or a gymnast. For instance, the trainer was showing us one particular trick, in which Lloyd was supposed to throw me up in the air. Without Lloyd's support, I was expected to tuck my body and then turn. I couldn't imagine executing a move like that.

However, the trainer was very patient with me. He realized he couldn't use the words "turn" or "flip." If he did, I would tune out. Little by little, I started to become interested in what he was trying to teach us, and eventually I began performing some of the moves on the floor, and even had fun doing them. Although some of these elements would prove to be impossible to accomplish on the ice, we did attempt a few. Because they are so acrobatic, however, we found doing them very difficult, and realized it would take considerable work and practice before they could be included in a performance or competition.

Although we will probably use variations of the moves we were taught by the Cirque du Soleil, I am not certain how many of them we will actually perform on the ice. I believe Lloyd and I are already pushing the envelope, and I can't see us doing much more than we already do. Moreover, as I get older, my goals are getting smaller. I don't want to try something stupid and cripple myself in the process. If I can't manage a flip over Lloyd's head, it is not something that I would consider to be a failure.

It was interesting to hear Rocky's reaction when he learned that we would be working with the Cirque du Soleil. At first he was curious and wanted to know more about what we were being taught. Then he became concerned about my safety. After a while, he didn't want to hear what we were doing at all, which bothered me.

"You are not interested in what I am doing?" I asked.

"Of course I am," he replied. "But I worry about you and don't want you taking chances."

"You, of all people, should know why I am doing this," I explained. "You take the same risks every time you and Calla step on the ice. This is our job and we have to understand that and let each other grow. And if I ever do fall on my head," I continued, "I hope that you will come to the hospital and hold my hand, even if you don't agree with what I am doing. That's what loving is all about."

Rocky assured me that he would be there for me, no matter what, and nothing more was said about it until a few weeks later. He came home from training and began to tell me how he and Calla were attempting something new on the ice. Although she wasn't injured in the incident and Calla had fallen on her head, the two of them tried the move again.

"Wait a minute!" I cried. "You are allowed to try new things to become a better skater, but I'm not? Calla could have kicked you in the head when she fell, and you could have been seriously injured." I wasn't really worried about what he and Calla had been doing, but was just trying to make a point. I think he got my message because the subject of my taking unnecessary risks never came up again.

Lloyd

Isabelle and I participated in numerous professional competitions over the years, and I would say that the majority of them have been shoddily run. It was a shock when we first began competing professionally, because in my fifteen-year career as an amateur, I had never competed under such abysmal conditions. Rarely, there may have been bad ice, but it was never compounded with poor or incorrect lighting and total disorganization. But that was because there was always someone on top of the game, ensuring the safety and comfort of the skaters. Not so in the professional world, where there are only a handful of promoters who produce competitions. Although each competition may have a different twist, they are all basically run by the same people. Hence, if a skater wants to compete, adjusting to the mediocre conditions comes with the territory.

Of course, there are exceptions, and one of these is the Canadian Professional Championships, which I believe is the best-run competition on the circuit. We participated in that event for four consecutive years, and each time it maintained a high standard. Even though I would get discouraged from the judging at the Canadian Pro (Isabelle and I came second for three years and finally won in 1997), the organizers always paid attention to detail and the skaters' needs. Furthermore, the network that televised the event was not dictating the competition. That is in direct contrast with American-run competitions, where all they seem to care about is television ratings. In the United States, I believe they are always looking for the story, whether it be Tonya and Nancy, Oksana Baiul getting into trouble, or how Katia Gordeeva is coping. The television producers will pick up on the story of the day and concentrate on that. The organizers, who only want to make money, do whatever the networks want and show little concern about the actual competition environment.

I also liked the World Team competition, which pitted country against country. But I believe I was partial to that competition because it was fun to participate in. When I turned professional, I missed the camaraderie of being on a national team, and I think the World Team competition is probably the closest one could come to re-creating that atmosphere.

If there was ever an event suited to our style of skating, it is the Fox Rock and Roll competition. As the name suggests, it is very upbeat and far more entertaining than any other competition we have entered. Judging was done by a panel of celebrities and the audience, who rated us through an applause meter. Isabelle and I won the event, and we looked forward to entering it the following year. Much to our disappointment, however, the organizers decided to restrict the event to singles skaters. It's too bad really, because a competition with that intrinsic level of entertainment was right down our alley.

The worst-run competition I have ever attended was the World Professional Skating Championships. Isabelle and I first competed in the event in 1994, and had a very dismal week. Expected at the rink at seven in the morning, we were sometimes held there until eleven at night. The competition was so disorganized that often the ice wouldn't be flooded before rehearsals. On one such occasion, Doug Ladret and Christine Hough took a terrible fall and had to withdraw from the competition entirely. The situation was appalling. What made it more so was that in many circles it was considered to be the epitome of competitions. The organizers, Candid Productions and owner Dick Button, would have you believe that winning the World Professional Championships was not unlike winning an amateur world title. It was a ludicrous notion, fed on the hype created by those associated with the competition. In reality, only its name set the World Professional Championships apart from any other competition on the circuit.

Because of our miserable experience there, Isabelle and I were very hesitant about returning. However, we decided to give it another try in 1997. That decision was a huge mistake. All week long, there had been delays of up to four hours in the rehearsals, and the usual bad ice. The pairs had been practicing under full lighting for the technical part of the program, and show lighting, which is basically spotlights, for the artistic segment. This suited Isabelle and me, because Isabelle, like many other skaters, cannot jump in spotlights. She tends to look at the ice to see where it is, and with spotlights, it is often difficult to see the surface—highly confusing and disorienting to the skater. That is one of the reasons we never include throws in any exhibition numbers, which are usually lit by spotlights.

The day of the show we arrived to find out that the lighting had been reversed. Now they would have spotlights for the technical, where most of us included our jumps, and full lighting and some spotlights for the artistic. We couldn't believe it. According to the organizers, however, it was too late to correct the lighting. We went out and skated the warm-up, and because Isabelle couldn't see, she fell three times on the throw. By the time we got off the ice, the two of us were very tense.

We had been performing beautifully all season, and had won almost every event that we entered. Now we didn't know what to do. There was no doubt that the lighting would severely affect our skating. It wasn't only Isabelle and I that were upset. All the pairs skaters who were participating in the event felt the same way. We decided to go ahead and compete, but every team skated below their accustomed level. This screwup cost Isabelle and me the title, which I believed we deserved that year.

When we skated off the ice, I was furious. I saw one of the organizers standing by the boards, and as a television camera caught my face, I said to him, "Maybe next time you will get it right." In an interview we gave to NBC, I explained what had happened. I wanted people to know what we had been through. Everyone thought I was angry because we fell and didn't win the competition, but that wasn't the case at all. Whenever I have sounded off like that, I am trying to let the public know that it isn't always the skaters who are lacking in credibility. Most of us perform to the best of our ability and the rest is out of our control. The organizers are supposed to be as professional as we are; they are expected to run the competitions with the proper lighting, sound, good ice, organized rehearsals—whatever it takes. When they mess up any one segment of the competition, it is the skaters who take the brunt. We look like the idiots because we fall. The promoters rarely own up to their mistakes. At that competition, I took it upon myself to tell the viewers. Not surprisingly, the interview never aired.

To make matters worse, the pairs segment was shown only on Canadian television. Nobody in the United States ever saw it. I don't know if that was because there were no Americans in that segment of the competition, or if it was because none of the teams skated well. It may have been that some of my critical comments were picked up by too many cameras. Whatever the reason, I think it was belittling to all the competitors. They invited us to the event, and then wouldn't even show it on television. It will take many years before I get over our treatment at that competition, and I doubt that we will ever return.

Isabelle

I have a theory about why the World Professional Skating Championships are so difficult for us. The promoters make far too big a deal out of the competition, and in the process they put too much pressure on themselves. People working there are under such stress because they really believe it is the biggest pro competition of the year. And when people are under stress, they make mistakes.

Lloyd and I have never had a good experience at this event. We always start practice late, and there seems to be one mishap after another. It is very frustrating to skaters who work hard to give a good performance. I normally don't say too much when things go wrong; that's usually Lloyd's department. However, even I got angry the last time we competed there.

Lloyd

When we were at the 1997 World Professional Skating Championships, I was surprised to hear Isabelle voice her displeasure. She is usually very calm and self-possessed. Because I didn't want anyone thinking badly of her, I asked my partner to calm down. "If it is necessary," I said, "let me be the one to speak in that regard. Everyone expects it of me anyway."

As an amateur, I used to have a very short temper. The television reporters would often hear my angry comments, or the cameras would follow me as I left the kiss-and-cry area in disgust. Now that I am older, I try to shrug off annoyances, though I will still speak up when I believe we have been mistreated or judged unfairly. Much of how well a skater does depends on adeptness at playing the game. That often means bowing down to the promoters and keeping your mouth shut. Unless you are an Olympic gold medalist (who could get away with just about anything), talent alone will not get you an automatic invitation to competitions and events. However, I will never change to please the powers that be. When I perceive that something is wrong, I am not afraid of expressing my views. And if people find me abrasive in the process, I hope they realize that my integrity will never allow me to be two-faced about any situation. Furthermore, I would never bring my dissatisfaction to the ice. When I perform, I am always 100 percent professional. Whether there be bad ice or poor lighting, I will still do my best to skate at my usual high standards.

Isabelle

I think almost all the professional competitions are run in a manner that would surprise most people. In fact, I can't remember participating in any event that I would consider ideal. When we were competing as eligible skaters, if something was wrong, organizers would stop the competition until the situation was corrected. Professional competitions are a far cry from that climate. Promoters and networks aren't in the business to help us skate better; they are there for the money and the television ratings.

Not every professional competition we entered, however, was a horrendous experience. Some were actually fun, and there were even a few that I looked forward to participating in. For instance, I always enjoyed competing at the Canadian Professional Championships. Unlike most of the other competitions, they were fairly well organized, and as a bonus, my family usually attended the event. Having my mother and brother at a competition always boosts my confidence. They have been my biggest supporters over the years, and whenever they are in the stands I feel like I can do anything on the ice.

When the Canadian Pro was held in Ottawa in 1996, there was a major snowstorm in Montreal, and although I had expected my entire family to attend, my brother had left messages at the hotel saying that he didn't think he would be able to make it. Luckily, my mother and Claude, her companion for the past few years, had arrived before the storm, and when I skated out for warm-up, I saw them sitting in the stands. I felt good that they were there, but I wished Dominique had been able to make it as well.

We were skating third that night. The second pair had just finished, and Lloyd and I were getting ready to step on the ice. I glanced into the audience again, with a faint hope that Dominique might be there. At that exact moment, I saw my brother running down the stairs to his seat. He had arrived just in time to see us perform, and I immediately felt stronger; I just knew I was going to skate well. And although we came second, it was the best Lloyd and I had ever skated at the Canadian Pro. We went on to win the event the following year, but even that performance paled beside the one we gave in 1996.

All of the World Team competitions we have entered also hold fond memories for me. To compete with skaters from your own country is a very special experience. I particularly enjoyed the years when our teammates were Kurt Browning and Josée Chouinard. In 1997, Kurt, Lloyd, and I didn't feel as confident as usual, and our practices weren't going very well. I am not sure why Kurt was having problems, but that was the year that Lloyd and I had difficulties with our training schedule. Josée was skating excellently at practice, however, and she acted as cheerleader to the rest of us. When we got down on ourselves, she'd say, "Come on, guys. I really think we can win this event."

The three of us weren't quite so optimistic. Canada had never won the World Team competition. In fact, we usually placed third or fourth in this event, where the Russian and European teams dominated. We told Josée that she had better not expect too much from us, but she jokingly said, "I am counting on you all to skate well and win. I want a new porch for my house and I need to pay for it!"

"The way we're skating, you'll have to wait another year for that porch," one of us commented. But Josée was relentless. She kept feeding us her positive attitude, and by the time of the actual competition, Kurt, Lloyd, and I were so pumped up, we went out and skated perfectly. Josée had to skate last. By that time, Canada was sitting in first place and was so far ahead of the other teams, it would have been almost impossible for us to lose. Suddenly Josée became nervous and looked to us for the same support she had given.

"Jo," I said, "our team already has so many points, it doesn't matter how you do. Just relax and go have fun." But she wasn't listening and felt as if the entire outcome depended on her performance. Although she had skated flawlessly for her first number, this time she didn't do as well and came off the ice disappointed.

"I'm so sorry," she sobbed. Kurt, Lloyd, and I hugged her and told her that if not for her upbeat attitude, none of us would have skated well. Despite what Josée thought about her own performance, our team won the event, and we credited our victory to her.

Until 1998, the regular professional competitions were mixed with pro/am events. Currently, almost all the competitions are a combination of professional and amateur. When Lloyd and I took part in them, however, they were a spin-off of the regular professional competitions. Although there were several we could have participated in, we only entered the odd one. I didn't like doing them because I thought the rules were very unfair.

There weren't any professional judges on the pro/am panels. Instead, they were ISU (International Skating Union) judges, who were only familiar with amateur rules, and they judged the competitions accordingly. This system so favored the amateur skaters that Lloyd and I were the only professionals ever to win a pro/am up until 1998.

The first one we participated in was called the Starlight Challenge, and was held in New York on an outdoor rink in Central Park. When we arrived, we discovered that we were supposed to have turning lifts in our program. No one had informed us of this rule prior to the competition, and we hadn't included any in our number. Right off the bat, we were deducted so many points. When you lose marks before you even begin to skate, it is certain you are not going to place very high in the standings. Then we lost even more points because we executed elements that were considered illegal by the ISU judges. To top it off, the late-November weather was freezing cold. That, along with the high winds, hampered our skating anyway. We placed last and I couldn't wait to get out of there.

When we were next invited to a pro/am competition, which was entitled the Ultimate Four, Lloyd and I tried to be very careful and follow the rules exactly. Even with meticulous planning, though, we learned that our number, "Tears in Heaven," was thirty seconds too long. Apparently, we were only allowed four minutes to skate. The organizers came to us during the last five minutes of practice the morning of the competition and told us we would have to cut the program. Nobody could show us the actual rule, but they assured us that we would lose marks if our program ran longer than the allotted time. So, in our running shoes, Lloyd and I walked through the number and attempted to cut some parts out. Whether our new version would match up to the music, we had no idea. Luckily, it did and we won the competition. Although we skated our best, I believe our win was partially due to the fact that the amateur couple, who was close to us in the rankings at the end of the first segment, gave an unexpected poor performance during the second half. The next time we competed at the Ultimate Four, we came second, and by then I had just about had it with pro/ams.

The technical segments of these competitions were all based on amateur regulations, and the eligible skaters had their entire season to practice that one number. When Lloyd and I were invited back to the Ultimate Four in the spring of 1998, we were given only a month's notice. Some of the people we would be competing against had actually taken their numbers to the Olympics in February. I wondered how Lloyd and I would look beside these skaters. I knew the entertainment aspect of our performance would be at it's highest point, but we hadn't had any time to practice and incorporate the necessary jumps and throws into our program. As it turned out, it was a moot point. We had just come off the Champions on Ice Winter tour, where I had injured my back, and would have been unable to compete regardless. But even if I was healthy and able to perform the technical elements, I would have refused to participate when I learned the rules for the artistic segment.

Although we would be allowed vocals to our music, all the other regulations were geared towards an amateur artistic program. We had to perform three lifts, a throw, and a side-by-side jump—elements that amateur skaters must execute. Deductions would be given for any moves that are typically performed in shows, such as the head banger and the Detroiter. We would also lose marks for executing our trademark chainsaw, or fly high–say bye.

It wasn't only Lloyd and I who were growing increasingly concerned about these pro/am events. Many professional skaters were turning them down because of their own bad experiences. When Jozef Sabovcik and Brian Orser placed fifth and sixth, respectively, at a pro/am in Japan, they both were reluctant to do them again. Scott Hamilton, one of the greatest skaters of all time, was deducted two points for performing a backflip at a pro/am. Tell me, where is the entertainment value in these restrictions? We turned professional to get away from rigid rules. The pro/ams were too reminiscent of our amateur days, and I wanted no part of them.

Lloyd

What none of us realized was that the whole face of skating was about to change. When Isabelle and I were competing as eligibles, there was a very big difference between amateur and professional skaters. They were two separate entities, worlds apart. As an amateur, money never came into play; the rules dictated that an amateur skater could not accept fees for competing. Whatever little I earned at an exhibition, or through the odd endorsement, was put into a trust fund that I was not permitted access to until I retired from the amateur ranks. One of the reasons I turned professional was that at last I would receive a paycheck.

That all changed when the Grand Prix was introduced. The ISU, which is now a client of IMG, the world's largest sports agency, and the agency that represents Isabelle and me, was trying to come up with a new slant on amateur skating. Professional skaters seemed to dominate television, and according to the ratings of our competitions and shows, were more popular than the amateur events. The ISU wanted to make their own competitions more interesting to the fans, but they were also attempting to keep eligible skaters from turning professional. Consequently, they decided to create a circuit of international competitions and pay the skaters to compete. Thus, the Grand Prix was born. Depending on how a skater placed, the eligibles could now make up to thirty thousand dollars for a single competition and fifty thousand dollars at the World Championships.

This was a dramatic change from when I competed internationally. If I won a major event, I received a pen set and a thank you very much. When the Grand Prix was first announced, I realized I could have been rich if I was competing in this era. However, I didn't begrudge the eligibles the money they would now earn. To me, the change was part of the evolution of our sport, and I was happy to still be around to enjoy the benefits of being a professional skater.

Gradually, the two worlds of skating were coming together. Amateurs could now make money, and more and more pro/am competitions were cropping up. Although Isabelle and I participated in a few of these events, we weren't pleased with the obvious favoritism shown towards amateur skaters. These competitions were run and judged by the ISU, and it was clear they wanted their skaters to shine. For Isabelle and me to get excited about these competitions, the judging panel would have to consist equally of amateur and professional people. Furthermore, rules would have to be fair to both ranks of skaters. However, the ISU wasn't changing its mind on how to run the pro/ams, and frankly, Isabelle and I didn't care. Not participating in a pro/am didn't mean much to us one way or the other. It wasn't as if we wouldn't be competing at all. Or so we thought.

In the fall of 1998, the majority of professional competitions almost disappeared entirely from skating. They were either dropped completely or transformed into an ISU-sanctioned open international, which translates as a pro/am event. These competitions would be open to professional and eligible skaters alike, along with skaters who wanted to keep their options open. This last group consists of people like Michelle Kwan, Ilia Kulik, Todd Eldredge, and Artur Dmitriev and his partner, Oksana Kazakova. They are permitted to compete and skate wherever they want, as long as it is an ISU-sanctioned event. Although you might not see these high-profile skaters at the World Championships, as long as they stick to the rules, they are considered eligible to compete at the next Olympics.

Prior to this decision, there had been a long struggle between individual promoters, agencies, amateur figure skating associations, and the ISU to control the market. As the popularity of figure skating exploded, everyone was after the money. I suspect that the major players decided to form an alliance and block out the competition. IMG, who produced some of the professional competitions, and also owned the World Championships, already had the ISU as a client. Then, from what I understand, IMG worked with Candid Productions, to organize a number of other professional competitions.

When I first learned of the decision to alter the format of the professional competitions, I was as confused as everyone else, but I didn't overreact. I thought it best to wait until I actually saw the rules for the events Isabelle and I may have been interested in competing in. Once I was certain of what I was dealing with, and had a chance to discuss the situation with Isabelle, we would make a decision based on the facts.

Isabelle

We weren't exactly sure who made the decision to change things. From what we heard, the networks weren't satisfied with the ratings of professional skating, so they went to IMG and asked what they could do to make the competitions more interesting. Since IMG already owned or was in partnership with the ISU, they decided to do pro/ams. They even turned the World Professional Championships into a pro/am.

All the rules in both amateur and professional skating were now different. For instance, Tara Lipinski won the gold medal at the 1998 Olympics and then announced she was turning professional. Michelle Kwan, who won the silver, decided to remain in the eligible world and compete again at the next Olympics. Michelle, unlike Tara, can compete at any competition she wants, as long as they are sanctioned by the ISU. She can join the professionals on tour and doesn't even have to compete at the World Championships. Tara, on the other hand, is totally banned from Worlds, Nationals, and Olympics. Not so much because she called herself a professional, but because she went on to compete at a non-ISU–sanctioned event. It is a very confusing state of affairs. And if the public is mixed up, I hope they take some comfort in the knowledge that most of the skaters are just as confused.

Lloyd

When I became familiar with the rules for the pro/ams, I immediately saw how one-sided they were, in favor of the eligible skaters. Of all the professionals, it would be the pairs that suffered the most. For the artistic numbers, the ISU were actually lowering the number of triple jumps allowed for the singles skaters. This, in fact, worked for the professional singles skaters, who, unlike the eligibles, weren't used to putting in nine and ten triples in one program. But as far as the pairs went, the rules had reverted to the Dark Ages.

I didn't have too much of a problem with the technical portion of the competition. It would have to be similar to what Isabelle and I competed with in 1994, and although we would have to include elements that were strictly amateur, I was confident that we were still competitive in that area. It was the artistic portion that I was having trouble with. This was supposed to be the *professional* side of the pro/am. However, the only indications that the ISU were complying with the professionals at all was that they were going to let us use vocals in our numbers and keep the programs to three and a half minutes. Everything else would be amateur-based.

Normally, Isabelle and I perform seven to nine lifts in a single number. Now we would only be allowed three. In addition, we would not be permitted to perform any moves that the ISU considered illegal. For a team like Isabelle and I, who have invented many moves that both excite and frighten the audience—moves that bring a crowd to the edge of their seats—this news was devastating. In my opinion, my partner and I have taken pairs skating to another level. We are doing lifts now that there are no names for. People call them adagio moves. This dates back to another era in skating, when pairs performed these types of moves in shows, on ten-by-twenty tank ice. Because there was no speed involved, the elements were far less daring than the ones we currently execute. We now perform adaptations of these moves on large ice at full speed, and have added a power and strength to them that would have been unheard of only ten years ago. However, because what we do isn't listed in the rule book, the ISU considers them illegal. If we went out and performed them, the judges would thrash us. First they would mark us down for not following the rules, then we would be punished even more for making it look as if we were laughing in their faces.

Isabelle

For us to go back and compete under the same regulations we did in 1994 was something we didn't need to do. Lloyd and I have worked hard the last four years to stand out in our field. We want to continue performing not only the moves we have created, but also the elements that are typically associated with professional pairs skating. Would the standard head banger now be considered too acrobatic? It was definitely created to entertain the audience, but it could also be looked at as a variation of the death spiral. Lloyd and I weren't certain if the judges would deduct marks for moves like these, and finally decided that the pro/ams weren't worth the aggravation. For the first time in our twelve years together, Lloyd and I wouldn't be competing when the fall season began.

Lloyd

If someone had told me that I would still be skating but not competing, I would have thought they were crazy. But Isabelle and I felt so strongly about the unfairness of the new opens, we decided to opt out of the 1998 competitive circuit.

During the season, we heard that our fans missed us at the competitions. Letters rolled into the editors of figure-skating magazines and daily newspapers throughout North America, complaining about our absence and the new skating system. Although we were touched by the comments, we didn't waver in our decision. Fans also missed seeing skaters like Brian Boitano, Nancy Kerrigan, Jozef Sabovcik, Rosalynn Sumners, and Katia Gordeeva. In protest of the pro/ams, these skaters and many others decided not to compete in the ISU-sanctioned events.

What was particularly hard for Isabelle and me was not competing at the Canadian Pro, which had also become a pro/am competition. We are Canadian and don't have many opportunities to compete in front of a home crowd. It was very disheartening.

I miss competing. I have always loved the competitive atmosphere and thrive on preparing myself for a competition. However, I don't miss the feeling I would have had if we had ignored our principles. I also know without a doubt that if we had attempted to compete, the stress of trying to comply with the rules and accept the biased judging would have been too much to bear.

Whether it was their intention or not, the ISU and IMG have successfully stopped many professional skaters from competing. Moreover, by creating their own events, they have ensured that all the money comes back into their pockets; one wonders at what cost to the seasoned skaters, their fans, and the credibility of figure skating in general. Only time will tell. I am not blaming IMG for this move. Isabelle and I aren't their only clients, and the eligible skaters will obviously benefit from this change. But what our agency and the ISU have done is basically eliminate Brasseur and Eisler from competition.

There has been talk about the creation of a new circuit for professional skaters only. If that happened, Isabelle and I may come back to the competitive arena. Not only do I miss competing, but I am not into letting the eligibles get the best of both worlds and leave the professional skaters on the outside. I hold no malevolence towards the eligible skaters. In fact, if this change to the rules had happened in 1994, Isabelle and I would have stayed eligible ourselves. There is no sense in amateur skaters turning professional now since more money can be made by remaining eligible and having the option to compete at the World Championships and Olympics, if they so choose. My problem lies with the fact that many professionals skaters are having to fit themselves into, or be totally shut out of, the sport that so many of us have dedicated our lives to.

Isabelle

I didn't miss competing at all during the 1998 season. Actually, I think it was good for me that I didn't have to worry about whether I had to land a jump or a throw. Furthermore, I was able to enjoy a few days off here and there—something I hadn't been able to do in a long time. I spent the night of the Canadian Pro, for example, with Rocky. We went to see one of the flower girls from our wedding, who was performing in a Christmas play. The six-year-old sat on my knee afterwards and showered me with hugs and kisses. I wouldn't have traded that moment for all the competitions in the world.

To compete before fifteen thousand people, and to have those fifteen thousand people happy that I was there, well, it would be nice for them. But if I had participated against my better judgment, I would have been unhappy. I never liked the pressure of competing to begin with. Even the professional competitions put a strain on my nerves. Since I don't agree with the politics of the pro/ams, why would I want to put myself through that agony? I love skating and I love to perform, and there are many venues where I can still do that; but I won't return to competition under those rules. I would much rather spend my time experiencing the simple joys that I have missed out on.

It is not that I totally disagree with this new system. Some people believe that bringing the sport under one rule might benefit it. But I believe it is impossible to tell at this stage. Furthermore, I respect our agency's choice to produce competitions of this nature. IMG encouraged us to participate in them. We refused, and now they have to respect our decision.

Whether Lloyd and I return to competition is uncertain. However, what is certain is that we have already proven ourselves many times over. My partner and I have had some great competitive moments in the course of our career. If we never have another, I can live with that.

CHAPTER FOUR

On the Personal Side

Isabelle

KATING has always come first in my life. When I was training to compete for World and Olympic medals, there was never any time to form and maintain long-term relationships. I would meet people and date, but since my focus was firmly on career goals, the new relationships would inevitably suffer.

For a time, Lloyd and I were involved. We began skating together in 1987, and two years later, we were dating. Halfway through 1991, my partner and I realized that although the affection we felt for each other enhanced our skating performances, our close relationship was beginning to hamper our training. Doing everything together, both on and off the ice, was just too much.

Away from the rink, we got on wonderfully. Not only did Lloyd and I have a deep friendship, but our feelings were very intense. To put it simply, we understood each other. On the ice was another story. Because we had grown so comfortable, we began to argue and criticize one another, in a way we had never done before. As time went on, Lloyd and I realized we couldn't continue in this manner. So because our skating was so important to both of us, we sacrificed our personal relationship.

This was a painful decision and an unhappy period in my life. There was no question that I loved Lloyd, and it took me a while to get over our parting. I believe our breaking up hurt him just as much, and for the next several months we avoided each other outside of skating. However, I always believed that if we were meant to be together at some point in the future, it would happen. In the meantime, we concentrated on our careers.

Lloyd

I could see how our dating was affecting the skating. The affinity we felt towards each other brought a unity between us that was obvious in our performances. But after a few months, we began fighting far too much. We made a choice, and as dispiriting as it was, I firmly believed it had to be done.

Isabelle and I were endeavoring to become World champions. That was our sole concentration, and at the heart of why we were together in the first place. In order to reach that plateau, everything else had to come secondary. To waste precious training time arguing about something that had taken place the day before, which had nothing to do with skating, was bringing us both down. Our decision to break up our personal relationship was difficult, but it was the right thing to do. Furthermore, I assumed Isabelle would be there for me in the future, should we ever change our minds.

Sometimes, when you are very comfortable and secure with a person, you automatically take them for granted. You shouldn't. But that's what I did. I just figured Isabelle and I would focus on our career for the time being. As far as our personal lives went, we would see where the road led us. I wasn't consciously thinking that we would get back together. But I guess in the back of my mind, I always believed that would happen.

Isabelle

In the summer of 1992, I began seeing Jean-Luc Brassard, a freestyle skier I had met the previous year. Jean-Luc and I had a very special relationship. I had just come off the Olympic and World championships, and wasn't satisfied with my performance at either competition. I was at a crossroads and truly wondered if I wanted to continue skating. Jean-Luc was a relaxed, easy-going person. Moreover, he was funny and he never failed to put a smile on my face. His optimistic outlook on life gave me perspective, which I needed during that confusing period.

Although we dated for a couple of years, we rarely saw each other during the competitive season; because we were both training for the 1994 Olympics, there was very little time. Jean-Luc went on to win the gold medal at the games, and his schedule became even more grinding. Even though he was still competing internationally, he was in great demand for commercial endorsements and appearances. In the meantime, Lloyd and I turned professional. Invitations to compete and perform poured in, and crushed any hopes that my own schedule might lighten.

By the spring of 1995, I concluded that my relationship with Jean-Luc wasn't working. Seeing each other once every couple of months wasn't enough for either of us. We were leading two separate lives, and it was unrealistic to call ourselves a couple. When we split up, there were no bad feelings. On the contrary, both of us were very sad.

Lloyd

I sympathized with Isabelle when she and Jean-Luc called it quits. Though it was apparent that she was unhappy, she never brought her troubles to the rink. Isabelle and Jean-Luc were exceptional athletes. Their careers took up most of their time, and they were unable to see each other as much as they would have liked. Jean-Luc traveled with us for a few days here and there, but beyond that, we didn't see him much during the winter season.

When their relationship began to sour, Isabelle tended to rely on me more than usual. If she was upset or had an argument with him, I would hear about it. But when she was on the ice, it was business as usual; our skating never suffered at all.

Isabelle

When I was in the middle of my breakup with Jean-Luc, Lloyd was also going through a troubling period in a relationship. Because the two of us couldn't seem to find happiness with others away from the rink, I began to wonder if it was because of our skating. Perhaps the sport was the cause of our failed attempts to find fulfilling and committed relationships.

One day, when Lloyd and I were discussing our problems, I asked him many questions. "Should *we* be together? Can the feelings we have for each other be called love? Although I never directly asked him whether we should resume dating, I wanted to know his thoughts. Lloyd and I shared time, emotion, and experiences every day. Maybe that's what true love was about.

Lloyd thought about my questions, then said, "No. I don't think that is it."

That night I wrote a letter to my dad. Since he had passed away, I would often commit my thoughts to him in writing. Somehow it made me feel closer to the man who had so influenced me. I asked him if skating was robbing me of the life I was supposed to lead. Was it preventing me from forming a relationship with one special person? Would I ever have someone to share my life with . . . someone who really cared about me? I appealed to Dad to guide me in the right direction. Two weeks later, I began a relationship with the man who would become my husband.

Aside from a divine intervention that I believed my father helped steer, Lloyd was the main reason that Rocky and I came together in May 1995. My partner was having a hard time with his current relationship and I was trying to help him cope. Rocky, who was also a good friend of Lloyd's, was on the Champions on Ice tour

(left)
Isabelle and Rocky walk down the aisle at their wedding.

(below)
Isabelle, her mother, Claudette, and nephew, Jonathan—Christmas, 1998.

D.M. SZABO

MARC EVON

(left)
Lloyd and Isabelle with a child
from the Children's Wish
Foundation at Dreams on Ice.

(below)
Lou-Anne Brosseau
(far left), Isabelle and Lloyd
with sponsor at Dreams on Ice.

MARC EVON

(above)
Cast of 1997 Dreams on Ice.

(left)
Lloyd fishing in Algonquin Park.

(left)
Lloyd with his mother and father at Sports Hall of Fame induction.

(below)
Lloyd and Isabelle with Guy Lafleur at Sports Hall of Fame induction.

D.M. SZABO

Rocky and Isabelle.

Isabelle and coach, Josée Picard, at a Chicago baseball game—July, 1997.

Lloyd with trainer Eric Lang on tour with Champions on Ice in California.

Lynda Prouse, Isabelle and Lloyd at a 1997 book signing for
To Catch a Dream—Burlington, Ontario.

(above)
Isabelle, Lloyd and Tom
Collins—1997 Champions
on Ice.

(left)
Lloyd and Steven Cousins,
Vale—1998 Christmas show.

Champions on Ice 1998 summer tour—some of the cast on a day off.

Lu Chen and Isabelle backstage at 1998 Champions on Ice summer tour. Someone had taped all of Isabelle's personal items to the wall of the dressing room.

with us. He too was helping to support Lloyd through this difficult time.

While we were on the road, Rocky and Lloyd often went out for dinner, or to a bar, while I spent time with various friends, such as Nancy Kerrigan. One night Lloyd wasn't up to socializing and suggested that Rocky join me and my friends instead. Rocky was reluctant since he had never been out with us before. Lloyd assured him we were fun to be with, and because Rocky had nothing else to do he joined my group.

During the evening, Rocky and I discussed how we could help Lloyd. Then the conversation turned to what I had recently been through with Jean-Luc. Before long, Rocky confided that his relationship wasn't going well either. We talked for hours, and within a couple of weeks, Rocky and I were involved.

As much as I had been wondering about what my future held for me in terms of a relationship, I really had no wish to become involved with anyone so soon after my breakup with Jean-Luc. My heart hadn't fully recovered and I thought it best to be on my own for a while. For the time being, I didn't want another boyfriend, and I definitely had no desire for another long-distance relationship. What did I get? A husband who lived in another country. Go figure.

Lloyd

Rocky and I had known each other for years, and our friendship dated back to before Isabelle and I teamed up. Although we were competitors, in the early days, we used to watch each other's programs while on tour. Each of us would cheer the other on, and when the skating was over, we would usually hit the bars. We had a lot in common then: both of us were young and single, and we skated in the same discipline. We worked hard and played hard. As we matured, we settled down in many respects, but still continued to seek out each other's company whenever we were both on the road.

At the time Rocky and Isabelle connected, I was in the midst of a breakup and was having some problems dealing with the situation.

Depressed, and seeking advice, I turned to Isabelle and Rocky separately. I guess my despondency opened the gate between them, and before long they were dating each other.

As much as I think they were concerned about how I would take the news, I wasn't at all upset that my two good friends were now involved. However, I was surprised. Knowing them both as well as I did, I wondered how two such opposite personalities could ever mesh. Isabelle was demure and very much the homebody. She tended to shun parties, and often preferred to stay in and work on her crafts. Rocky, on the other hand, liked the city and the nightlife. Truthfully, I never dreamed their relationship would develop into anything serious.

Isabelle

Although Lloyd never told me how he felt about me and Rocky dating, I could sense that he was surprised. Moreover, he acted as protective as a big brother. "Make sure he doesn't hurt you," he said. "If he does, come and see me." I don't believe he thought we were serious, but then again, neither did Rocky or I.

In the beginning I kept telling Rocky that I didn't want a long-distance relationship. It was one thing for us to be on tour together, where we had months to see each other on a daily basis, but when the tour was over, I couldn't imagine returning to a situation that mainly played out over the telephone. Rocky didn't pressure me, and although we spent most of our time in groups, we got to know each other fairly well during the rest of the tour.

Towards the end of June, I made plans to spend three days with Kristi Yamaguchi in San Francisco, where the tour finished in July. I postponed my flight home and looked forward to spending time away from the rink with Kristi, who had become a close friend. A few weeks later, Kristi informed me that she had been booked for a photo shoot during the days we were supposed to spend together. She apologized, but wouldn't be able to see me while I was in town. Since I had planned to stay at her place, I didn't see the point of remaining in San Francisco myself and decided to go home after the tour ended. When I told Rocky that I had canceled my plans, he suggested that the two of us go to Napa.

At first I thought it was a great plan. But the night before we were scheduled to leave, I panicked. Rarely had we been alone together on the tour, and here I was, about to spend three days with someone I had now convinced myself was a stranger. I asked Lloyd what I should do.

"Don't worry," he calmly stated. "If you aren't enjoying yourself, just tell him. He will take you to the airport and you can fly home."

Fine for him to say. Lloyd never had any reservations about being blunt with people. I tried to picture myself explaining to Rocky, "Excuse me, but I am really not enjoying your company. Can I go home?"

Filled with misgivings, I went to Napa with Rocky. Happily, my fears were totally unfounded. Rocky and I had a wonderful time. We felt very comfortable with each other and laughed at everything. By the end of our little vacation, we decided our relationship was well worth maintaining. And even though we were living in separate countries, we kept it going over the summer and saw each other as much as possible.

That October, Rocky and I were walking around downtown Philadelphia, close to where he lived, when we spotted a jewelry store. Just for fun, we went in and I tried on some rings. We had been talking about how nice it would be if we could spend more time together, but had made no definite plans. Although we had discussed marriage, I thought our engagement was at least a couple of months away.

A week later, we both competed at the World Team event, and flew back to Philadelphia. It was on a Saturday—October 21, to be exact. Rocky and I spent the day at his apartment and were planning to go to dinner that night. That day, I found him and his family acting peculiar. For instance, both of Rocky's parents dropped by the apartment. His mother's presence wasn't unusual, but his father always worked on Saturday. Yet his dad came in, gave me a big kiss, and left. Then Rocky insisted that I dress up for dinner. Usually, he didn't care what I wore.

Rocky continued to act a little strange during dinner. It was almost as if he was nervous. Then, sometime after we finished eating, he arose from his chair, came over to me, and knelt down. I realized his intent and said, "Here? In front of everyone?" He just smiled, then asked me to marry him. I didn't have to think twice about my answer.

Lloyd

Isabelle and I were at Halloween on Ice when she told me that she and Rocky had been discussing marriage and were thinking of getting engaged. Up until that moment, I hadn't realized how intense their relationship had become. Suddenly, I became anxious about my own future with Isabelle.

It wasn't our skating career that worried me. In all the time we have been together, there was never a doubt that we would remain partners on the ice. It was how my personal relationship with Isabelle would be affected that bothered me. A part of me still thought that at some point in the future, she and I might resume our relationship as a couple. I knew that if I didn't speak up then I would have to forever hold my peace, so to speak. However, I could see how exhilarated she was, and I didn't want to put a damper on her joy. No matter how I felt at the time, I wanted Isabelle to be happy. How could I be a true friend if I was not pleased at the bliss she seemed to have captured? So I decided to say nothing about my own uncertainties.

When she and Rocky formally announced their engagement, however, I experienced an overwhelming sadness. I did my best to hide it from them, but the realization that my relationship with Isabelle was never going to be the same hit me hard. It was like a door slammed shut on me. I believed that even though we would always be friends, Isabelle and I would never again be able to share every hardship and happiness that we had outside of skating. The first person she would call in a crisis wouldn't be me anymore. Nor would I reach for the phone to talk to her as regularly as I used to. She would have someone else in her life now.

For so long, even though I have had girlfriends, my career had always come first. In fact, I have lost relationships because I wasn't willing to make even a small sacrifice to my career in order to appease anyone else. But it was something that had never worried me. Because I had such a good friend in Isabelle, I reasoned I didn't really need someone else outside of skating. I had it all with her.

Isabelle

I told Lloyd about my engagement the weekend it happened, calling him the day after Rocky proposed. At first, he didn't believe me. When I assured him that it was true, he sounded more shocked than pleased. Afterwards, when we met face-to-face, he didn't mention my engagement. Even later, when I told him the wedding date was set for August 10, 1996, he didn't act excited. Instead, he asked me if I was certain I was making the right move. His reaction bothered me.

I wondered if Lloyd was upset because he thought maybe he and I should be together. After some thought, I dismissed the idea. After all, we had been apart as a couple for several years. When we split up, we had left our relationship to fate. Later, when Jean-Luc and I parted, I asked Lloyd if what he and I had could be called love. He didn't seem to think so. I assumed then that if we were still unsure of our feelings after all that time, a personal relationship between us truly wasn't meant to be. After writing the letter to my dad, I met Rocky and it was like a sign to me. As our relationship progressed, I continued to "speak" to my father, asking him to take my hand and guide me. I believe he did that, and led me to become Rocky's wife. I was so filled with happiness and wanted my best friend to share in it.

I still had to tell my mother that I was engaged and I wanted to break the news to her in person. Originally, I hoped that Rocky would accompany me. However, he was unable to get away, and so a week after we became engaged, I went to see her on my own.

When I told my mother about our engagement, she looked pleased, but she didn't seem surprised. When I questioned her, she stated that she already knew. She had been to see a psychic in May, who had informed my mother that my brother's wife, Josée, was going to have a baby and that the child would be a boy. Josée was pregnant at the time and went on to deliver my first nephew, Jonathan. The psychic then told my mother that her daughter had a new boyfriend, who was twenty-nine years old (which Rocky was), and predicted that we would marry in the near future. I remember when Rocky and I began to date, my mother had asked me his age. But she hadn't told me then of the psychic's premonition. I guess she didn't want to influence me.

Lloyd

As the plans for Isabelle's wedding began to unfold, I could see our relationship changing daily. My partner and I were growing further apart and I started to feel left out of her life. When we began the Champions on Ice tour the following January, no longer was it Lloyd and Isabelle. It was now Isabelle and Rocky, who was also on the winter tour. They were fast becoming a single unit, and I felt like the third wheel. Although I am not saying that Isabelle and I spent every moment together while we were on the road, we often shared meals and conversation. Whenever either of us had a problem, we automatically called each other. Now, if Isabelle needed to talk, she turned to Rocky. And she spent all her free time with him.

When Isabelle first announced her engagement, I wasn't worried about our career. However, in time, I saw her interest in skating decrease as her plans of marriage and a new life increased. It was a natural occurrence for her, but I had some difficulty in dealing with it. As I've mentioned, skating had never taken a backseat to anything in my life, and as it dropped on Isabelle's priority list, I experienced some anxiety.

I was also concerned that she was marrying someone who lived in the United States. Isabelle had always said that she never wanted to leave Quebec. Now I wondered what she would decide. The implications of our living in two different countries and trying to train were staggering. Pairs and dance partners have to maintain both physical and mental proximity. Without the two elements in sync, a career together can quickly disintegrate.

Isabelle

Lloyd was growing more distant; it was as if he was consciously stepping away. I understood why. In the past, if I had a personal problem, I always looked to Lloyd for help. And he was always there for me. Even when I dated Jean-Luc, it was Lloyd I relied on. Now I had to become less dependent on him. I couldn't marry one man, yet go to another with my problems. It wouldn't be fair to either of them.

It was a puzzling time for all of us, and in the beginning it was difficult to know where we stood with one another. Lloyd denied that anything was disturbing him, but I could see him withdrawing. He avoided spending time with Rocky and me, and often would barely acknowledge my presence if Rocky was by my side. If we were all at the same social function, I would approach Lloyd and he would say, "Maybe you shouldn't be talking to me because Rocky is here." I would tell him that it didn't bother Rocky, and then ask him to join us. Lloyd would refuse. After a while, Rocky began to feel that Lloyd was shutting him out.

It was almost as if Lloyd was angry that I was getting married, and I didn't know what to do about it. I wanted to keep him and Rocky happy, but at times I felt as though I was in the center of a brewing storm. I realized that my marriage would affect Lloyd, but I had an adjustment to make as well. For the past eleven years, I had gone to him for everything. It wasn't easy to turn that off. Nevertheless, when I made the decision to marry Rocky, I also decided to share my life with him. Our future together as husband and wife depended on it.

Lloyd

I truly wanted Isabelle to be happy and tried hard not to show her my distress outwardly. However, as her wedding day approached, I found myself growing more despondent. Isabelle was so busy, and other than Rocky's asking me to be in the wedding party, I wasn't involved at all in her plans. I do remember, however, Isabelle asking me what I thought about her wedding dress and veil. I told her the outfit was beautiful, and for a few minutes I felt good knowing that she still valued my opinion.

Isabelle planned much of the wedding while we were on tour in the winter and spring of 1996. Rocky and Calla weren't on the spring tour, so my partner spent much of her time on the telephone with her fiancé. Whenever she had a couple of days free, she would fly home to attend to details. It was hard on her in two ways. Skating was taking away from the time she needed to plan her wedding, and the wedding plans were affecting our skating. There was just no time for her to train or to correct anything that needed fixing. Moreover, any personal life that we once shared vanished during those busy months. Other than the three minutes we spent together on the ice, I rarely saw or talked to her.

I didn't look to anyone else to replace Isabelle's friendship while we were on the road. I am a tough person to understand, and many people find me insensitive and brusque. But that's not the real me. Isabelle knows that I can be abrupt or do stupid things, but she also recognizes me for who I really am. It took years for us to become that familiar with each other, and I was not willing to give up that part of me to someone I didn't trust. Many people in skating are superficial, and trying to become close to anyone else just didn't seem worth the effort. As a result, I spent most of the winter and spring tours alone.

Isabelle

Lloyd wasn't involved in our wedding plans because Rocky and I chose to do everything ourselves. We didn't even ask our parents to help out all that much. We didn't want other people to run around on our behalf. Instead, we hired a wedding organizer. Although she provided us with a few names and some other information, most of the organizing fell to Rocky and me.

Like any other wedding, ours was a lot of work. First we had to pick a date and a location. We wanted the ceremony to take place in the summer of 1996. Because the Champions on Ice spring tour wasn't finished until late July, we had a certain time frame to plan in. However, I wasn't sure where the wedding should take place, in the United States, where Rocky's family lives, or in Canada, where mine lives. In order to be fair to both our families, we contemplated holding it somewhere in between the two cities where we lived. The more Rocky thought about it, the more he wanted the ceremony to be held in Montreal. It would be easier for me, he said, and since many of his family members had never been to Quebec, he thought they would enjoy the experience.

We began to look at quaint hotels on the South Shore, where I lived, hoping to hold our wedding reception in that setting. Again, we took into consideration the many guests who had never visited Montreal. We decided that it would be more convenient and enjoyable for them to be in the city. With that in mind, we made the rounds of downtown hotels. As soon as I saw the Ritz Hotel, I knew our search had ended.

Finding the church for the ceremony was almost as easy. I wasn't too familiar with most of the churches in the core of Montreal, but I knew that Notre Dame was breathtaking. However, it was booked for the weekend we had selected. Then the wedding organizer suggested St. Patrick's Basilica. When I stepped inside the magnificent cathedral, a shiver ran up my spine. With its vaulted ceilings and intricate stained-glass windows, it seemed magical. There was no doubt in my mind that this was the place I wanted to be married in.

Because I was booked for three tours in the first half of 1996, I tried to get as much accomplished as I could before leaving in early January. We even chose the menu in December. The staff at the Ritz thought we were deciding on the dinner far too soon. Under normal circumstances, menu selection doesn't take place until the month before the wedding. But I didn't care. It would be one less detail to think about.

I also purchased my dress early. Mom and I had been shopping in late November and I was trying on various gowns. I had no intention of buying one that day, but wanted to get a feel for what was available. I chose first from a catalogue and the various dresses were then brought out for me to try on. There were so many styles that it was mind-boggling, and I wondered how brides before me ever knew when they found the right gown. Then the salesclerk brought out a dress by mistake. It was one that I hadn't even noticed in the catalogue. Although on the hanger it didn't look as nice as some of the others, I told her I would try it on anyway. When I slipped the garment over my head, it seemed to transform into a thing of floating beauty. It was perfect. Mom wanted me to wait at least a week before I bought it, in case I saw another dress I preferred. I agreed, but later that day I returned to the store. It was senseless to keep trying on other dresses, I reasoned, when I had already made up my mind.

Although I had much of the basics covered by the spring of 1996, I recall a few phone conversations with Rocky when I was close to hysteria. There was just so much to do. Because I was on the road, I wasn't able to keep an eye on things the way I would have if I was at home. For instance, I hadn't liked the chairs at the Ritz. They were too shabby, considering the elegance of the hotel. When I mentioned my concern in December, hotel staff assured me that new ones had been ordered. However, two weeks before the wedding, they still hadn't replaced the old chairs. I began hunting for material to cover the old seats, then had to find someone to make over two hundred slipcovers in ten days! I also wasn't happy with the florists I had hired. With very little time left, I was forced to hire someone else to create the floral arrangements.

As busy as I was, I don't believe it affected my skating performances. When I am on the ice, I concentrate only on the job at hand. After the tour, however, I didn't think about skating at all. In fact, that year, Lloyd and Lou-Anne planned Dreams on Ice without me. They told me not to worry about the show, realizing how overloaded I was with the wedding.

During the last stage of the tour and just before the wedding, Lloyd was particularly helpful. Normally, when we have been on the road that long, we both get pretty moody. It is very easy to become irritable with someone when you have been around them constantly. But Lloyd saw how much stress I was under, and he dealt calmly with every situation. It was actually peaceful for me to go and skate with him. If I became too upset or anxious about the wedding plans, he would quietly sit and listen to me vent. He knew what I needed and he gave that to me.

If there was one thing that I wished during this exciting period of my life, it was for Lloyd to experience the same happiness I was feeling. For so many years, we shared everything. Ours was a team—a partnership. If one of us was going to the Olympics, the other was going. If either of us fell on the ice, it reflected on both of us. Our names were as one, and together we had been through the same joys and sorrows. Now it felt strange for me to be stepping into a new phase of life without him.

Lloyd

For two people who have been intertwined for so long, the happy ending would be to have both experience every life-changing event with each other, or at least at the same time. Obviously that is not possible in the real world. Marriage was the furthest thing from my mind. Other than a brief engagement that I never really thought out, I had never seriously entertained the idea of a lifelong commitment to one person. Skating always got in the way. That was my choice, and I was very comfortable living my life relatively unattached. Now I had to accept and respect Isabelle's choice.

I decided early on, however, not to bring a date to her wedding. Instead, I invited a friend whom I had met on the spring tour. She knew most of the skaters who were going to attend, and she was also aware of how I was feeling. It made it easier on me to have someone there who wouldn't require a lot of my attention. I realized the day would be emotionally difficult for me, and I just couldn't handle a boyfriend-girlfriend scenario.

Before Isabelle's wedding, I made an effort to stay busy both emotionally and physically. On the evening before, I invited our mutual friends out on the town. Not only did it help Isabelle to know that her guests were being entertained, it was also my way of avoiding sitting around and thinking too much.

Isabelle

There were many good friends that I could have asked to be in my bridal party. However, I finally chose five women, who each in her own way was special to me: Julie Marcotte, who was my maid of honor; Marie Josée Fortin, Josée Picard, Kristi Yamaguchi, and my sister-in-law, Josée Bolduc, acted as bridesmaids. Kristi stayed at my house the night before the wedding, and she was great to have around when my nerves were frayed.

Kristi had also planned a shower for me while I was on tour. She and U.S. pairs skater Jenni Meno organized the surprise party and invited all the women skaters. Unfortunately, my grandmother, who had been ill for some years, passed away and I went home for the funeral. Since this happened when my shower was scheduled, the girls had to scramble to reschedule it. The only time they could get everyone together was between shows at the rink. They apologized to me because of the setting, but I was grateful. My friends had put much thought into surprising me and I was touched by their caring.

I was very stressed out on the day of my wedding. I had worked so hard to ensure that everything would be perfect, and now I was a nervous wreck. I was also a little scared. Although I was very much in love with Rocky and excited about our future together, marrying him was going to be a huge change for me. Like every other bride, I couldn't help wondering if I was making the right decision, because I didn't want to regret it later.

That morning, I awoke with my head in a cloud, and would continue to feel that way for the rest of the day. The next few hours passed so quickly that it was a good thing plenty of pictures and videos were taken. Without them, I doubt if I could have remembered many of the details.

I was adamant about wearing "something old, something new, something borrowed, and something blue." Not wanting to press my luck, I had it all planned out. The "old" would be a garter that Lloyd had once caught at a wedding he attended and given to me years before. My dress was the "new," and my undergarments were "blue." For the "borrowed," my sister-in-law, Josée, loaned me a pearl bracelet, which she had dropped off to me that morning after I returned from the hairdresser.

In the limo en route to the church, I looked down at my arm and noticed I had forgotten to put on the bracelet. "Oh no!" I cried. "We have to turn around and go back!" There was no way I was going to proceed without the borrowed item. My mother and brother were with me in the car, and couldn't believe how I was overreacting.

"We're not going home," Dominique firmly stated as my mother tried to calm me down.

"Well, I can't get married without it," I stubbornly replied. The limo driver, who was a woman, had been listening to me carrying on. By an amazing coincidence, she was wearing a pearl bracelet that was similar to Josée's. The driver told me that if I promised to return it, she would loan me her bracelet. I gratefully took the piece of jewelry from her and fastened it around my wrist. Now I was ready to get married.

When I stepped through the doors of the church, I was astonished to see so many people inside. Because St. Patrick's Basilica was such a large cathedral, we had decided to open the ceremony to the public, and announced our nuptials in the local newspapers. I later learned that including the two hundred invited guests, hundreds more had come to witness the ceremony.

As I walked down the aisle with my brother and mother on either side of me, I thought of my father. Although I had "talked" to him the night before, I had been too busy that day, but I sensed his presence in the church. And before I met Rocky at the altar, Mom, Dominique, and I lit a candle in his memory. My family wanted everyone to know that we were thinking about the man we missed so much.

For much of the ceremony, I was in a daze. We had chosen a priest who spoke both English and French, believing a bilingual ceremony would be fair to both families. Somehow, however, the priest got away from the order of the service we had planned, and Rocky and I became confused by what he was saying. When he finally told us that we were husband and wife, and added that Rocky could kiss me, he spoke in French. Rocky didn't understand, and just stood there. "Kiss me," I whispered. "It's time." Rocky looked at me as if to say, "Oh, are we married?"

Lloyd

As Isabelle walked down the aisle, I thought she had never looked lovelier. The reality of the situation also struck me. This was happening and it wasn't going to change. I kept telling myself that things would remain the same between Isabelle and me, but deep inside I knew I was fooling myself. Our friendship would always be there because we had experienced so much together. At that moment, though, I believed that she and I were at a fork in the road and headed in different directions.

When Isabelle and Rocky spoke their vows, so many thoughts ran through my head. I had taken it for granted that she and I would be together someday, because until she met Rocky, no one had come into our lives that seemed to make that much of a difference. Isabelle had boyfriends and I had girlfriends, but nothing had worked out on either side. As much as I tried to have other relationships, I believe I was always comparing them to the one I'd had with Isabelle. If I was going to be romantically involved, I wanted someone exactly like her.

Years ago, I began to call Isabelle by the nickname "Fred." We had been teaching a very young pairs team, and although the boy's name was Frederique, everyone called him Freddy. Because he was so little, we thought he was very cute and, in my opinion, he also had a great name. I thought Isabelle was like Freddy in that she was cute and little, and from that moment on I dubbed her "Fred." It was my own personal endearment towards Isabelle. At her wedding, as she and Rocky sealed their marriage with a kiss, I recall thinking this was the end of her being "Fred" to me. I may have looked calm on the outside, but inside I was overcome with emotion.

Isabelle

After the ceremony was over, Rocky and I stood outside the church amid a sea of floating bubbles and well-wishers. Then, after some pictures were taken, my new husband and I left for the hotel, where again we stood for more pictures.

At the reception, Rocky and I danced to an original piece of music composed and played by Karl Hugo. Karl had written it specifically for our wedding, and it was very moving. Then the party began and I think everyone enjoyed themselves. I know I did. However, the evening passed much too quickly. Because there were so many guests, I didn't have the chance to talk to everyone as much as I wanted to. I hope they all understood.

Later in the evening, Lloyd and I danced. People seemed to step back and watch us, but maybe that was because they were so used to seeing us perform together. I looked up at him and saw glistening tears in his eyes. And then it struck me how I was definitely going somewhere else without him, and that both our lives would be so different from that day on. Everything was going to change.

Lloyd

On the steps outside the church, I made a conscious effort to stand away from Isabelle. This wasn't our moment. It wasn't a skating event. This was Isabelle's special day, and there was absolutely no reason for the spotlight to be on me.

After the reception began, I danced with Isabelle, and again I became very emotional. As we moved around the floor, we spoke about the past and the future. Isabelle told me that it would never be the same again. Her words reinforced what I had been dwelling on, and reassured me that I wasn't crazy for thinking that way. She felt it too. That dance was symbolic and very bittersweet for me. It was my way of saying goodbye to the past and hello to the future.

CHAPTER FIVE

After the Wedding

Isabelle

A S ROCKY AND I sat in the San Francisco airport, I began to wonder if we would ever have a honeymoon. We had driven to Philadelphia after the wedding, and from there we were supposed to fly to San Francisco and then on to Hawaii. However, one of the plane's engines malfunctioned, and we were forced to land in Chicago. Hours later, we eventually were on another flight to San Francisco, but only after I lost Rocky in the airport.

Quite a few people on the original trip were honeymooners, who were also traveling to Hawaii. When we had to land in Chicago, everyone was pushing to get onto another flight. We were all running from one end of the airport to the other. At some point during this frantic commotion, Rocky was trying to book us on a flight, and I was in an entirely different place, attempting to get us on another one. When I went to find him, he was nowhere in sight and I spent the next half hour trying to locate him. Needless to say, my nerves were close to the edge.

We finally boarded the plane and arrived in San Francisco at about three in the afternoon. However, because we were late, we missed our connection to Hawaii. Since another plane was leaving at eight that night, we put ourselves on standby. Unfortunately, we couldn't get on that airplane, and so the airline put up the thirty of us who were trying to get to Hawaii at a hotel for the night. That was another disaster!

The hotel was falling apart, and during dinner, one couple found a beer-bottle cap baked into their veal scallopini. Another of the newlyweds told us that someone had walked into their room in the middle of the night. We couldn't wait to get back to the airport, and arrived at seven in the morning, to go on standby once more. Hours later, we boarded a plane to Hawaii, and I breathed a sigh of relief. Maybe now we could start our honeymoon.

My relief was premature. We were only in the air ten minutes when the pilot announced that he was having trouble with one of the engines. The captain advised us that he was dumping fuel and heading back to San Francisco! I thought, this is it. Rocky and I were going to be forced to spend our honeymoon in the city where it all began for us. Fortunately, however, we got onto another flight, and at last we were on our way to Hawaii. When we finally made it to the islands, we slept for three days straight.

Lloyd

When I heard about the problems Isabelle had had on her honeymoon, my automatic reaction was to ask her why she hadn't called me. In the past, if either of us had any troubles while we were away from each other, we immediately got in touch. Then I remembered. She was married. From now on, any problems she had would be worked out with Rocky. That was normal and the way it should be. I would just have to get used to it.

While Isabelle was on her honeymoon, I went to Los Angeles to participate in the taping of a Disney skating production of *Beauty and the Beast*. Also starring in the show were Viktor Petrenko, Katia Gordeeva, Shae-Lynn Bourne, and Victor Kraatz. The producers had originally requested Isabelle and me as a team, but because the event conflicted with Isabelle's honeymoon, we thought we would have to turn the invitation down. I asked Isabelle if she minded if I took the part on my own. She had no qualms about the idea and thought participating would be fun for me. It was. I skated with three other girls in a seven-minute segment. With rehearsals, costumes, and set changes, the show took thirteen hours to get on tape. The long hours didn't concern me though. I was busy doing the thing I loved best and it kept me from stewing about the future.

Isabelle

I thought it was great that Lloyd did *Beauty and the Beast* on his own. Under other circumstances, it may have bothered me not to have been skating with him. But because I had just experienced such a big event in my own life, I was glad he had something exciting to look forward to.

We had both been offered the role, and when I couldn't do it, the producers wanted to invite another team. They thought that because we were a pair, one of us wouldn't be able to skate without the other. I called our agent and asked her if there was a chance Lloyd could go on his own. I didn't see the point of taking a job away from him because I couldn't be there. Lloyd skated with three other girls, and I thought his performance was superb.

One of the hardest decisions Rocky and I had to make was where we were going to live once the honeymoon was over. I had always said that I would remain in Montreal for the rest of my life, but then I hadn't counted on marrying an American. Rocky was very understanding about this dilemma, and we continually debated the pros and cons of living in either country. However, just when we thought we had reached a decision, one or both of us would change our mind. For a time we were certain that our home would be in Quebec. Then a week later, we decided on New Jersey. Not long after, we began considering various locations between our home cities. We even purchased a lot in New Jersey, then canceled it a month later.

We finally decided to be realistic. At the time, Calla was pregnant, and Rocky wasn't sure how long he would be skating for a living. He thought he might have to find another job, and since he didn't speak French, it would have been difficult for him to get one in Montreal. We also realized that financially we would be better off in the United States. So with a lump in my throat, I said goodbye to Canada for the time being.

Living in the States was so strange at first. I would get in my car and head to the store to buy groceries, but wouldn't be sure how to get to my destination. Everything was unfamiliar to me. And I missed my family terribly. I still do. I can't get together with everyone on a Saturday night like I used to. At times, even now, I can be in New Jersey or anywhere else in the world and think, I shouldn't be here. I should be with my family and friends. I especially miss seeing my coach, Josée, on a regular basis.

When I begin to feel melancholy, I remember that I wasn't home all that much to begin with. And now I actually spend more time with my brother and his family than I ever did in the past. Dominique purchased my house in Montreal, and whenever I am back in the city, I stay with him, my sister-in-law, and my nephew. My mother is spending more of her time in Florida, and so I would still have to travel to visit her, whether I lived in Montreal or not.

Gradually, I adjusted to living in the United States. However, I still think about returning to Canada. Maybe Rocky and I could purchase a summer home in Quebec, or perhaps one day we could move back there on a permanent basis. I don't know what the future holds, but a decision to move back would have to be good for both of us.

When I relocated to New Jersey, I realized my move was going to have a definite effect on the way Lloyd and I worked. Obviously we would have to make many changes in our training habits. In the beginning, I believe it was more difficult on me than on Lloyd, because in order to train, I would have to travel. We were used to training in Boucherville with Josée and Eric, and for quite a while we continued that routine. It wasn't easy. On top of traveling to shows and competitions, I now had to book flights just to train. But being married to Rocky was worth the sacrifices I had to make.

I had also realized that skating had indeed taken away my personal life. Yes, it had given me much in return, but what it offered wasn't what would be important to me in years to come. I didn't want to end up thinking, Oh, I had a great skating career, and made some money, but where do I go from here? I wanted to have someone to share my life with. For me, having that one special person means more than skating for another five years or having lots of money in the bank.

Although Lloyd and I had a lot to work out in the first year after I married Rocky, we eventually organized ourselves in a way that was satisfactory to both of us. We found a rink in Philadelphia that was comfortable to train in, which put Lloyd more at ease. He began coming to New Jersey and would stay with Rocky and me. Little by little, we all inched our way towards a middle ground that we could live with.

I know my marriage was hard on Lloyd. Neither of us knew how it was going to affect us personally and professionally. We were close friends, but now he had to stand back and figure out what his role in my life would be. I had to do the same. If I had car problems in New Jersey, I wasn't going to call Lloyd in Quebec. I am sure he felt left out and it must have hurt him.

Because there were so many feelings to deal with, my marriage to Rocky took a toll on his relationship with Lloyd as well. Although they remained friendly with each other, I don't think they will ever be as close as they once were. As various situations arose, I often found myself in the middle, feeling loyalty towards both men.

It took us all quite a while to adjust. There were many stressful moments. But because we all cared about one another so much, we made our new relationships work.

Lloyd

After Isabelle and Rocky's honeymoon was over, I had to face the fact that we now lived in different countries. She was eight hours away by car, and we would have to figure out a way to train. Initially much of our time was spent on the telephone, attempting to organize ourselves for the upcoming season. I have never been very good at handling details over the phone. I like to deal with people face-to-face and tell them directly how I feel about an issue. Suddenly, because there was no time, or one of us had to go and do something else, our schedule wasn't coming into place. That was something that never would have happened in the past, when we always made the time.

For the first year, whenever we spoke, we seemed to discuss only business. I had never viewed our friendship as work-related, but that is what it became. Isabelle's priorities had changed. Marriage was at the top of her list, then her personal life, then skating, then me. Nurturing a personal relationship takes time, but the way things were going, Isabelle and I would have had to slot it into our already disarrayed schedule.

Isabelle's marriage didn't affect our talent as a skating team, but for a while, it most definitely affected the pre- and post-skating. Trying to figure out where and when we would train was a major job in itself. Eventually we found a facility in Philadelphia and, to some extent, it made both our lives easier. However, there were still problems to work out.

We tried to keep everyone's career individual but doing this successfully was impossible. My professional partnership with Isabelle would sometimes get tangled in her marriage, and in the beginning, I resented it. If we had an argument about our skating, she told Rocky, who would naturally side with his wife. He would form an opinion, which would affect the way we all communicated.

In the past, our professional relationship had never extended beyond Isabelle and me. None of our competitors knew what was happening between us on or off the ice. Now they did. It wasn't only the two of us working out our problems anymore. And the more people that were brought into our problems, the more difficulty we had in resolving them.

This also worked the other way. If Isabelle mentioned a problem she was having at home, I would inadvertently form an opinion about what Rocky should or shouldn't be doing. With the professional and personal scenarios overlapping, there seemed to be friction among us all the time.

Because of the tension, Rocky and I didn't always get along, and there was no question that Isabelle was caught in the line of fire. Sometimes, things would get so bad that I would feel like removing myself entirely. Then she would only have to deal with a marriage. Attempting to be in two places at once was a big strain on Isabelle. She was trying to balance her career and her personal life, and it was a constant struggle for her. And because I didn't want to lose her friendship, or our career together, I coped as best I could.

Often, the longer one is in a situation, the easier it becomes. Since Isabelle's marriage, we are now back to our usual organized routine as far as skating goes. I also made some life changes that helped me to empathize with Isabelle and Rocky. In 1997, I purchased a house on the outskirts of Montreal. Furthermore, I formed a relationship with a person whom I thought I could share the rest of my life with. Unfortunately, it wasn't meant to be. However, because we lived together for quite some time, it helped me gain insight into what Isabelle and Rocky must have gone through during their first year of marriage. Trying to bring two lives together is difficult enough without adding the pressure of a career as hectic and public as ours. Now, whenever we face a problem that involves the three of us, Isabelle, Rocky, and I sit down and discuss it. By communicating in an open manner, we all get along much better.

I still miss what Isabelle and I once had and sometimes wonder about how things could have been, had we not broken up all those years ago. I will never know if it was a mistake, but because of our decision, we went on to become World champions. Had we stayed together on a personal level, we may not have realized that dream.

Isabelle is happy and we're skating better than ever. That's all that really matters. Although we don't see each other as much as I would like, our relationship is solid. We have a better understanding now of the roles we play in each other's worlds. It's a secure feeling, strengthened by the knowledge that although our lives may change, our friendship remains steadfast. It took me a long time to adapt, but Isabelle is back to being "Fred" in my heart. To tell you the truth, she never really left.

CHAPTER SIX

Tom Collins Champions on Ice Tour

Lloyd

EARLY IN THE NEW YEAR, when most people are content to stay at home, many professional skaters are cramming suitcases and saying goodbye to family and friends. We know that other than the occasional hurried visit in a strange city, we probably wouldn't be seeing our loved ones again until sometime in the summer.

Touring season is a time of mixed feelings for the professional skater. Although it is beyond a doubt the most grueling time of the year, many of us eagerly anticipate getting back on the road. Performing nightly before a live audience is a heady experience. There is nothing like a standing ovation to lure you back to the life of hotels, room service, buses, and airplanes.

Two of the most high-profile tours today were created by promoter Tom Collins. Both shows are called Champions on Ice. Tom's winter tour was established in 1996 and currently runs from early January to mid-March. The spring tour, which marked its twentieth anniversary in 1998, starts in April and finishes at the end of July.

Originally called the Tom Collins Tour, the event was meant to coincide with the end of the World Championships. If the competition was staged in North America, the tour replaced the ISU circuit and featured only amateur skaters. As the event became more successful, Tom began sprinkling his shows with professional skaters. Now there is a good combination of both eligible and ineligible skaters on the spring tour. The winter tour, on the other hand, was originally designed to feature professional skaters only. It fell during the time of year when amateurs were busy with national and world competitions. When all the rules changed in 1998, allowing eligibles to opt out of international competitions, the 1999 winter tour saw a few of these skaters on the program.

When Isabelle and I were competing at the amateur level, it was considered a sign of success if Tom Collins invited you on his postseason tour. Although we had won the Canadian Nationals in 1989, and hoped for an invitation then, it wasn't until we won the silver medal at the 1990 Worlds that we were asked to participate. I later learned that the delay was the result of the usual politics involved with skating.

In those days, I was considered to be outspoken and rebellious. The Canadian Figure Skating Association (CFSA), which Tom often looked to for input on which skaters to ask on the tour, thought I might not behave in the manner befitting one of their Canadian skaters. However, Tom and I spoke after the competition, and I promised him that my skating performances were never affected by my moods. Skating my best at all times, regardless of my physical or mental state, is what I do—guaranteed. However, convincing Tom was not necessary. He had seen Isabelle and I perform at the Worlds and had already made up his mind to extend an invitation to us. Since then, we have participated in all his tours, and I have never broken my promise to him.

In 1991, IMG took me and Isabelle on as clients. IMG produces the Stars on Ice tour, which features professional skaters and travels throughout the United States for much of the winter. At the beginning of April, another version of the tour crosses Canada. Although it plays at the same time as Tom's winter tour, Stars on Ice performs in the larger cities, while Champions on Ice plays the smaller venues. After the American run of the IMG tour is finished, Tom's spring tour begins and revisits many of the cities where Stars on Ice played.

When we turned professional, IMG wasn't too excited about us touring with Tom Collins. The promoters of the various tours are in competition with one another, and if you are aligned with one group, you do not tour with the other. But part of our initial agreement with IMG stipulated that Isabelle and I be allowed to continue with Tom Collins. He was there for us when I couldn't get an agent to return my phone calls, let alone sign us to a contract. Thus, we are the only IMG clients who participate in the Canadian version of Stars on Ice and the two Tom Collins tours. To illustrate how unusual this is, if Isabelle and I were hockey players, it would be like our playing for the Boston Bruins and the Montreal Canadiens at different times of the season. Our situation is unheard of, but one that we are thrilled with.

Isabelle

Although I don't know Tom Collins on a personal level, I am very familiar with what he is like to work with. Tom is a personable man who knows what he wants from his skaters. In some respects he is strict, and won't put up with any nonsense or bad behavior from the group. But he has a deep understanding that we are not machines. While he asks a lot from us, he realizes that problems can develop and he is open to our feelings as individuals.

When my grandmother died in the summer of 1996, I told Tom that I would perform in the show that night, but advised him I would have to leave immediately afterwards for the funeral. Not only did Tom assure me it wouldn't be a problem, he told me to take off as much time as I needed. It was the same in 1997 when I developed pneumonia. I was well enough to perform, but Lloyd and I thought it best to cut back to one number instead of our usual two. Tom was very concerned that we were going to skate at all, worrying that I was pushing myself. He asked me to promise to tell him if I found it to be too much.

His interest in the skaters' physical and mental well-being goes beyond an employer wanting the best from his employees. Tom really cares about us as people. We reciprocate by giving him the best performances possible.

Lloyd

Although Tom began organizing his own tours in 1978, he had been involved with the European ISU circuit since the late sixties. Born in Kirkland Lake, Ontario, Tom and his two brothers, Butch and Harris, skated with Ice Follies and Holiday on Ice. Since he was a skater himself, it gave him an understanding of us that some other promotors don't have. Tom also worked in merchandising and marketing for various rock stars including Bob Dylan, Neil Diamond, John Denver, and the Moody Blues. Because the figure-skating tour is remarkably similar to a rock music tour, Tom was extremely knowledgeable in what it took to put a successful one together. An astute businessperson, Tom knows how to motivate people and is incredibly adept at remembering details about people's lives. He has been around skating for a long time and doesn't forget anyone that he meets. One of the things I most admire about him is that he treats every skater on tour equally. Whether the person is a celebrity or not, each of us is shown the same degree of respect. We like to think there are no stars on the tour. However, certain skaters believe that because they have won an Olympic gold medal or a World Championship, they should be given special privileges. After a day or two on Tom's tour, they soon realize that everyone is equal in his eyes.

I have always been very honest with Tom, and consider him to be a friend rather than an employer. If I had something to complain about, I wouldn't hesitate to tell him. Many skaters are nervous about voicing their opinions to him. Tom is a powerful man in the skating world and they are afraid of losing their jobs, or not being invited back on tour. I could never understand these fears. He is always willing to discuss any situation, and if he feels a suggestion will improve the show, Tom is very open to considering it. I have also found him to be a compassionate listener to any problems I might have. Whether they had to do with my personal life or my professional career, Tom was there to help me in whatever way he could.

A generous person, Tom has advanced the sport through his many donations to the United States Figure Skating Association and other grassroots organizations. For several years now, he has also been one of the sponsors of Dreams on Ice. Gestures like these have made him the success he is today. He can be as hard-nosed as any businessperson I have ever met. However, he is so down-to-earth, it is impossible not to like him.

Isabelle

Tom runs the tour and travels with the skaters. If we have to take a six-hour bus journey, he is there with us. If we are traveling by airplane, and are seated at the back of the plane, so is Tom. He would never ask us to do anything that he wouldn't do himself. It's one of the reasons the skaters feel close to him.

Although Tom's son, Michael, helps him out now, for years that role was filled by Harris, Tom's younger brother. As producer/director, Harris was involved in every aspect of the tour, but he passed away from a massive heart attack in June 1996 at the Chicago United Center just before the afternoon performance of a two-show day. I was in the dressing room with some of the other women skaters. We had received our five-minute call when a couple of the girls and Nicole Bobeck's mother entered the room, crying. Nicole's mom had been walking with Harris, who was preparing to get the skaters on the ice. She informed us that he had collapsed and his condition looked serious. We didn't learn of his death, however, until we were on the bus after the second show. I guess Tom thought that some of the skaters' performances would be affected if they knew Harris had died. We had many young skaters on the tour who hadn't been through this kind of tragedy. Although it was difficult for all of us, some took it very hard. Giving them time to adjust before the next performance was probably a smart move.

Lloyd

Harris was going to be missed by all the skaters. Like Tom, he was a good friend to many of us and always called a situation the way it was. He was only forty-nine years old when he died but, as many people reflected, at least he was doing what he loved best when it happened.

Since Harris passed away, Tom's son, Michael, has moved into the management sector of the tour, and has several competent people working with him. Generally, Michael is aware of the entire production and acts as a backup for Tom, in case he has to be away from the tour. Michael and I get along very well, and have been known to go out and enjoy a few drinks together. He also plays golf. Since that sport has become a major passion of mine, Mike and I often take to the links with skaters like Todd Eldredge, Alexander Zhulin, and Todd Sand.

Aside from management, there is an expert crew involved in setting up each show. Headed by Paul Hendrickson, who has been with the tour as long as I've been participating in it, there are approximately ten individuals who handle the lighting, sound, and all the technical aspects of the show. The crew travel separately from the skaters and arrive at the venue early to organize the production setup. Because they remind me of my friends outside of skating, I enjoy being around the crew guys. There is not a prima donna among them and I like that.

For the past couple of summers, I was able to spend even more time with this group than usual. While on my motorcycle, I often followed their trucks from city to city. Although I only travel like that for the last two weeks of the tour, it has been a saving grace for me. During that period, I don't have to step onto a crowded bus or plane once. It also gives me the opportunity to get away from every-one else and be on my own for a while.

After three months of being with the same people day in, day out, a person needs space. At least I do. We eat, skate, play, travel, and even shower together. Frankly, whether the skaters are my friends or not, I get as sick of their company as I am certain they do of mine. By the end of the tour, we have all had it.

Riding my bike alone is almost like a vacation. I leave the city we have just performed in, and with a grin on my face say, "See you guys in the next town." If the weather is on my side, I ride for as long as seven or eight hours at a time, loving every minute of it. I avoid fol-lowing the skaters' buses and instead trail the crew trucks. Not only do they know the best roads to take, they are also familiar with the truck stops along the way. Getting off the bike and joining the crew guys for a coffee and some laughs is one of the highlights of my trips.

Isabelle

Because I hate being away from home for such a long time, I don't look forward to going on tour. Putting off the inevitable as long as I can, I tend to leave things until the last week. Then I try to do every-thing at once: see the doctor, get my hair cut, go to the dentist, clean the house. I wind up a basket case with the stress of it all.

When you are leaving home for three months, and then you are only back for a few weeks before heading out for another three months, there are so many things to think about. First, you can't leave your house unattended for all that time. Plants need to be watered and mail has to be taken in. If a pipe bursts and no one is there to notice, your house could be a wreck by the time you return. When I lived in Montreal, I hired someone to come in and look after things. Now that I live in New Jersey, if both Rocky and I are away at the same time, his mother looks after our place. I am far more comfortable with this arrangement. If there is water in the basement or something goes wrong with the swimming pool, I know she will call someone in to look after the problem.

I also dread packing. In fact, I am a bear when it comes to that chore. After years of going on the road, however, I almost have it down pat. You may think that packing for such a long period of time is almost impossible. But it is really no different than if you are going away for two weeks. You would pack enough for one week, wash the clothes, then wear them again. I do the same. For example, I bring eight pairs of socks with me and wash them when they are dirty. We don't stay at the same hotel long enough to send out our laundry, but we usually have a washing machine and dryer at the rink.

I also bring basic clothes that are old favorites, and can be mixed and matched with each other. However, since we are traveling to different climates, and usually start in the cold-weather zones, I take more clothing with me at the beginning of the tour. As we get to the warmer parts of the country, I get rid of the coats, boots, and sweaters. I either ship them back, or if Rocky visits me on tour, I send them back with him. If I forget certain pieces of clothing, I will send for them, or purchase something new. The key to it all is organization; otherwise, you would go crazy.

Lloyd

Touring has become such second nature to me that I can pack for three months in less than thirty minutes. I'm familiar with what the weather is like in each of the cities we'll be performing in, and therefore know exactly what type of clothing to bring. Since we work east to west on the Tom Collins tours, in the winter I start off with heavier clothes. I look at the schedule to see when I'm going to have a couple of days off, and pack only enough to get me to that point. Then I try to fly home. If for some reason that won't be possible, I will pack more. Since we often go from wearing boots and jackets in Chicago, New York, and Boston, to donning shorts and sandals in Los Angeles, I ship the cold-weather clothing home. I am also aware of how long I can go between laundry sessions, and gauge my outfits accordingly. Packing doesn't bother me a bit; I could do it with my eyes closed. What I have trouble dealing with is attempting to get my household in order before I leave.

Having someone to look after the mail, clean my house, and pick up messages is one of my biggest headaches. I don't like to leave my place empty, and prefer to have someone live in on a full- or part-time basis. Unless you have family nearby, which I don't, you have to hire a responsible and mature person to take care of household matters. Once I have made those arrangements, I am more comfortable leaving the house.

During the season, I am usually home for a two- or three-week period after Tom's winter tour ends, and before Stars on Ice begins. When Stars on Ice finishes, Isabelle and I fly directly to the United States and join up with Tom's spring tour, which has already opened. Because of this back-to-back schedule, I try to cram six months' worth of appointments into the few weeks I'm at home. There is no routine, other than the frantic attempt to get everything done before I have to leave again. It can become so hectic that I often look forward to getting back on the road just for some rest. On tour, our schedule is regimented and organized. Moreover, it revolves only around skating. Other than handling my mail and phone calls from home, there is little else that I have to attend to of a personal nature.

Isabelle

All travel arrangements are handled for us while on tour. Everything is so meticulously planned that we don't even have to worry about our luggage. When the skaters arrive, we are assigned a number that remains ours for the duration of the tour. The identifying number is then attached to our bags. When we are ready to leave a hotel room, we simply place our luggage outside the door at an appointed hour. The next time we see it is in the following city. Our skates, of course, are carried with us. We could manage if a piece of luggage was lost along the way, but if our skates were to disappear, we might as well go home.

Since we usually don't have any group numbers on the Champions on Ice tour, there really aren't any detailed rehearsals. Each skater, or team of skaters, performs one or two of their own numbers, which have already been well practiced. We also perform in a thirty-second opening, which introduces the skaters to the audience. The brief closing is also nothing more than an appearance by the entire cast, allowing us the chance to give one last bow. Neither of these segments takes much effort. However, it is still necessary to arrive at the tour a few days before it opens, when our numbers are run through for the technical crew, who are there to organize the lights and music.

Once we have performed in our first show, which always begins on the East Coast, we move out to the next city. Sometimes, however, we stay in one hotel for a few days and journey to various venues in the surrounding area.

All of the skaters' traveling is done by bus or airplane, depending on the distance between cities. The buses are comfortable and similar to those used by tourists. On the winter tour, we require only one bus. However, on the spring tour, when there are at least twice as many skaters, we need two vehicles.

We spend so many hours traveling, I find it necessary to keep busy during the long treks. Otherwise I feel as though I am wasting time. If I'm not reading, I work with my hands, either embroidering, knitting, cross-stitching, or more recently, quilting. I am always on the lookout for new crafts, and a couple of years ago, when I was in Calgary, I found myself in a quilt shop. The storeowner offered to teach me the intricate craft, but because we were on tour, I didn't have the time. The following year, when I was next in Calgary, Kristi Yamaguchi and I called the shop and arranged for a private class. Then I taught U.S. pairs skater Jenni Meno, Russian Olympic gold medalist ice dancer Oksana (Pasha) Grischuk, and Chinese World champion Lu Chen. Between the four of us, we purchased a portable sewing machine and took it with us on tour.

Many of the female skaters like to do crafts on the road. Even one of the men has taken up knitting as a hobby. On the 1998 winter tour, Rudy Galindo decided he wanted to make a sweater for his nephew. Rudy already knew how to knit but had forgotten some of the stitches. So I told him if he went to the wool store and purchased the materials, I would knit the same pattern in a larger size for my own nephew. Since we would be working on the sweaters together, I would be able to help him out. Rudy and I wiled away hours working on our projects. Some of the men laughed at him, but Rudy didn't care.

People pass the time in various ways while on the buses. Some skaters catch up on their sleep, while others play cards or work on their computers. Most of us chat to those sitting near us, who are usually closer friends. However, I've seen many skaters talk for hours on a cell phone to someone who is thousands of miles away. This usually occurs when the person has recently formed a relationship outside of skating, and is desperately trying to keep in touch. I can imagine what their phone bills must be like at the end of the tour because I do the same trying to keep in touch with Rocky!

Once in a while people bet with each other on the distance between two cities. I can recall when Lloyd bet Tom Collins a thousand dollars that the next destination was at least seven hours away. Tom insisted it was only five. Lloyd had the advantage, however, because he had taken the same route on his bike the year before. It actually took us nine hours to get to that particular city. We arrived twenty minutes before the show was scheduled to open. By that time, everyone but Lloyd was on edge. My partner was happy he'd won the thousand dollars.

There is nothing worse than being late for a show. While you are trapped on a bus or elsewhere, realizing that the audience is taking their seats can make the strongest of us tremble. Racing to get into makeup, costumes, and skates, with only a few minutes to spare can be the most harrowing experience.

The closest we have ever cut it was when we were traveling from North Dakota to Utah. Our bus was supposed to leave at 11:00 a.m. to take us to the airport, where we were scheduled to board a noon flight. This would give us plenty of time to be ready for the evening show, slated to start at seven-thirty. That morning, we checked out of our rooms as usual, and boarded the bus that was waiting outside the hotel. We had just settled in when Michael Collins announced the flight had been delayed. He informed us we wouldn't be leaving for another hour and a half. Rather than wait on the bus, the skaters got off. Without hotel rooms, we just walked around the area and returned to the bus at the designated time.

Back on the bus, Michael again told us we were in for another delay. He didn't know when we would be leaving, so advised the skaters not to stray too far. Thank goodness it was a nice day. We spend so many hours on a bus as it is, it would have been terrible to have to sit in one and not go anywhere. Instead, we waited outside. Some of us talked, while others played games or cards. We were there for hours. Finally, at 5:00 p.m., Michael told us that he had hired a few small jets to fly us to Utah. The problem was, the planes could seat only four skaters at a time. So we rushed to the airport, where the first four skaters in the lineup of the show boarded and left for Utah. Some of them actually put on their costumes and makeup in the jet. They made it to the rink with fifteen minutes to spare. The rest of the cast left in order of appearance. Because Lloyd and I were skating in the second half of the show, we didn't arrive until intermission was over. Needless to say, there was no opening that night.

Lloyd

Sometimes we spend as little as an hour on the bus—a half hour to the rink and a half hour back to the hotel. Then there are the days when we are on the bus for as long as ten hours. It all depends on the distance of the venue we are performing in. Every now and then, however, other factors come into play. For instance, if we are finished in one city and the venue we are next scheduled to perform in is available early, Tom's people will try to get us out ahead of the original schedule. If there are no flights available, you can bet we're going by bus, no matter how far away the venue is. The success of these tours depends on precise scheduling, and if we can get into a venue earlier than expected, it's one less worry for the organizers.

Tom tries to provide the skaters with as much comfort as possible while we're on the road. Even though the buses are equipped with fairly modern amenities, including vcrs for the person who wants to watch a movie, they are still buses and the hours spent on them can be mind-numbing.

Some people sleep the entire trip, but I find it difficult to have anything more than a quick nap. Because of my size, I need four seats if I want to sleep. Someone like Isabelle, who is tiny, can snooze quite comfortably on two seats. On the winter tour, we usually have more room to stretch our legs, but the spring tour is so crowded with skaters and their friends that we often have to double up. When you're traveling for five hours with another person literally breathing down your neck, it's brutal.

One year while we were on the spring tour, one of the two buses broke down during a long trek. The bus I was on had to go back and pick up the passengers from the disabled vehicle. Everyone was forced to double up, and there weren't nearly enough seats. Because Tom is so generous, he lets the skaters bring people on tour with them. Some invite their boyfriends, girlfriends, coaches, or close family members. On this outing, several of the skaters had to stand while the visitors sat. It was ridiculous.

Overcrowding often occurs anyway. Some skaters will bring their entire families from city to city. A whole entourage will board the bus, each person expecting a double seat. I have seen buses so jammed that Tom will take some of the skaters off and send them ahead in a cab. In my opinion, certain skaters abuse Tom's hospitality and take advantage of his good nature. Nobody minds if someone's parent or friend rides on the bus once in a while. But for heaven's sake, show some consideration to the other skaters.

In all the years I have been participating in Tom's tour, I have never taken my parents. They visit me in cities where I'm performing, but they don't ride on the bus, and if they are going to come and see me, it is because I have a couple of days off after a show. They watch me perform, and then we can spend some time together. Occasionally I have brought a friend on the bus. But never more than one person at a time, and I ensure that he or she sits next to me and doesn't take someone else's seat.

Many of the skaters get as annoyed as I do when we are forced to sit shoulder-to-shoulder with each other, especially at the end of the tour, when the majority of us are irritable and fatigued. However, very few people will speak up. It's usually left to the ones who are more vocal, such as me. If someone is getting on my nerves, whether it be the skater, their parents, or their friends, I tell them.

After a show, on our way back to the hotel, the bus is stocked with juice, coolers, beer, wine, and junk food. It's like a moving canteen. We tend to be more relaxed then, and many skaters will walk the aisles chatting to one another. Often, groups sit together, discussing their performances over a glass of wine or a beer. Although I will socialize if the mood strikes, I tend to spend this time on the bus alone.

These long hours in the middle of the night give me the perfect chance to think. I reflect on my life, both past and present; it's almost a form of meditation. However, sometimes I overthink, and when that occurs, I can become anxious about whatever I'm mulling over. That's when I get up, open a beer, and seek the company of another person.

Isabelle

A few of the female skaters on tour travel with their mothers. Surya Bonaly, Nicole Bobeck, Michelle Kwan, and Tara Lipinski are usually chaperoned by a parent, which I understand when a girl is fifteen or sixteen. But is this necessary for an adult?

When Tara participated in her first tour a few years ago, I could see why she needed her mom. She was young, and neither she nor her mother was used to touring. I sympathized with them and tried to help out as best I could, remembering that when I started out, things were easier because Lloyd was with me. He wasn't afraid of anything and I looked to him for security. Even though he was much older, he always included me in his plans and I knew that if I went with him, I came home with him after. If I had been on my own that first year of touring, I probably would have been lost.

Lloyd

New skaters on Tom's tour won't be given their own hotel room, or a choice of roommate. Management assigns everything. On my first tour, I shared a room with American skater Mark Mitchell. At the time, I had no idea who Mark was, or if I wanted to room with him. As it turned out, Mark was just as wary of me. Luckily, we got along very well and roomed together for the next four years. Although we have extremely different personalities, we kept to our own routines and respected each other's space. Our arrangement worked so perfectly that the organizers kept us together until Mark left the tour. By then my new contract stipulated that I have my own room, which I wanted, knowing it would be difficult to find another roommate as ideal as Mark.

Tom always puts the skaters up at the best hotels in the cities. Obviously, if we are in a small town in the Midwest, the facility may not be as grand as one in New York City. However, after being on tour for so long, it doesn't really matter if I am staying at the Ritz Carlton or the Holiday Inn. A hotel is a hotel. The only things I care about is whether the room is clean and the bed is comfortable, and if there is enough water pressure to take a decent shower. I am in a hotel to sleep. It is not my home. I spend so many nights in hotels that I truly am sick of them. If I had friends in each city that I travel to who would ask me to stay with them, I'd accept the invitation in a second. Many people don't understand this, and seem almost wistful when they realize we often stay at five-star hotels. But I swear, I couldn't care less.

Isabelle

Up until 1994 I shared my hotel room. Most of the time I was with Nancy Kerrigan, but I have also roomed with Kristi Yamaguchi. Because we spent so much time together, I made two very good friends. When I turned professional, however, I was given my own room, and the only person who shares with me now is Rocky.

Lloyd

No two days are ever the same on tour because of traveling. If we are in one city but are fairly close to the venue, we may leave the hotel at two-thirty in the afternoon, to get to the rink for three-thirty. Because there is minimal traveling involved, this is classified as a show day.

Once we arrive at the rink, practices start around four-fifteen and continue until seven in the evening. If everything has gone according to schedule, this will allow each discipline thirty minutes on the ice. The order in which skaters practice is rotated each show day. Once in a while, however, our bus arrives late because of heavy traffic, or there's a glitch in the production setup. On those days, we are often permitted only ten minutes on the ice, just to get the feel of it. Even worse, the ice is sometimes not good because it has been put in the day before; the paint comes through and the surface has to be reflooded. In that case, we have no practice at all and have to perform "cold turkey." There are a number of things that are out of our control with respect to practice, and these occur at least 25 percent of the time.

Once practice is over, we mostly scatter and do our own thing. Because we are at the venue until at least 11:30 p.m., and are skating in only one or two numbers at most, there is a lot of downtime. On Tom's tour, we travel with a full set of weights, bench machines, sit-up machines, two bikes, two StairMasters, two treadmills, mats to work out on, pinball machines, a pool table, a Ping Pong table, and a dartboard. This equipment is transported on trucks to the rink and set up before the skaters arrive. When we are not skating, most people work out or play the games.

I have my own schedule when I arrive at the venue and rarely deviate from it. I work out immediately for an hour and a half on the weights and machines. Following this, I eat from the buffet that is set up daily, then I practice. After practice, I have about an hour and a half to relax before the show begins. Every day changes a little because of the rotation of the thirty-minute practice sessions.

Then there are travel and show days combined, when we have a 5:00 a.m. luggage call, with the bus leaving at seven and the plane by nine. If everything goes according to plan, we will land at noon, and go to the hotel, where we may have forty-five minutes to unwind. Then we are back on the bus, headed to the venue. Those are the hardest days because we have to be up so early and then perform that evening. We often arrive back at the hotel by midnight, only to have to arise at 6:00 a.m. for another travel/show day. Sometimes we have seven of those days in a row. That can mean seven different cities in seven different states. That's when it can become so tedious that you actually forget what city you are performing in.

Isabelle

On a show day, I usually wake up around ten-thirty in the morning. Most of the time, we have been traveling the night before, so I like to sleep in. By the time I get dressed, it is lunch time, so I either order room service or go downstairs to the hotel's restaurant. Then I return to my room, pick up my skate bag, and head for the bus. On a travel day, we leave by nine in the morning and journey by bus or plane. By the time we arrive at our destination, if it is early enough and we are not performing that evening, Tom often takes us all out on the town. If we have a show to put on, however, we normally head right over to the rink.

Once every few days, the skaters are given time off. On those days, I may go sight-seeing or shopping, attend sports events, or visit friends in town. If Rocky is on tour with me, it is much more enjoyable to share these activities together since we don't have much time during the off-season to spend in this way. When I'm not in the mood to go out, and we are in a warmer climate, I lie by the hotel pool and sleep or read. I hardly ever see Lloyd when we do have a free day. He's either visiting with friends, at the gym, or the golf course.

Lloyd

I love golf. I set aside any free day I have on tour, weather permitting, to play the game. A group of us plays together, and I think most of us took up the sport as a release from the tensions of the tour. For me, it grew into a favorite pastime, and is something I pursue as often as I can.

Other than golf and skating, most of the guys I play the game with don't have very much in common. In fact, we rarely go anywhere else together. Various groups form on tour, and depending on their interests, the skaters usually associate themselves with one or many. For instance, the Russians tend to group together, while the North Americans usually stick to one another. Professionals often go out only with other professional skaters, while the eligibles tend to call other eligibles to spend the day with. Certain women prefer other women for company, as in Isabelle's group, where most of them like to make crafts. Then there are the married skaters, who socialize with other married couples, and the gay skaters, who tend to pursue their interests separately. While we all mix very well as a large group, on a day-to-day basis, bonds form with those you have most in common with.

For example, I like to work out, so I go to the gym regularly. Rudy Galindo shares my love of exercise, and we often go to the gym together. Working out by myself can be boring, but when I have someone else along, especially a person with Rudy's comical personality, it's fun.

We even have groups of people who only get together to dine at a specific restaurant in a certain city. Because we have traveled for so many years, we each have our favorite eating places. For example, when we arrive in Dallas, about ten of us immediately make plans to dine at a restaurant we discovered ages ago. The group of us may not go out together at any other time on the tour, but for sure we'll be together for one night at that particular restaurant.

Isabelle

One group I'm definitely not involved with is the golf group. I hate golf. I tried to play the game a few times, but I just couldn't get the hang of it. I was even offered free access to a golf course one summer, after someone saw me try to play on television. My personality changes when I play golf. I get too angry at myself. There is something about the sport that frustrates me. More often than not, I'll finish my game by throwing the club as far away as I can.

Although I will work out at the rink, I am not nearly as fanatical about it as Lloyd. I have my schedule and I try to stick to it, but I'm not going to spend every moment in the gym. For some people, it's a weight issue. I can remember the first year we were on tour, Lloyd gained twenty-five pounds. So now he has to watch what he eats and exercise regularly. I'm the opposite. I have a hard time keeping my weight up. Sometimes I'll go through an entire day and suddenly realize I only ate a bagel or a croissant at breakfast. Then I have to sit down and eat something more substantial, because I can't afford the weight loss.

Lloyd

Although I join different groups for certain outings, for the most part I tend to be a loner while on tour. The only person I try to see regularly is Isabelle. If she is free, I eat lunch or go out somewhere with her. When Rocky is on the tour, however, I am usually by myself. I actually find it easier that way. When I am away from the rink, I don't like to talk about skating with anybody else other than Isabelle. Unfortunately, most people in this sport find nothing else to talk about.

When I'm on the bus and don't speak to anyone for four or five hours, I have heard it said that some people think I'm a snob. Others wonder why I am so quiet and don't want to join in on the fun. I shrug them off, with assurances that nothing is the matter. And it isn't. I just don't want to be rude. If I told them we had nothing in common and I found their discussions to be trite at times, I'm sure they would be offended.

When I first began touring, I used to be the most obnoxious of them all. I wanted to be included in every activity and conversation. But time and experience have taught me that quiet is better. Being the life of the party is not who I want to be. I still love to go out and enjoy myself with a group of people now and then. Most of the time, though, I prefer my own company.

Isabelle

If not for Tom's tour, I probably wouldn't be such good friends with Kristi and Nancy. Before the tour began, we were only acquaintances. Then, because we were skating for different countries, we were able to see each other only on tour. Every year we are out on the road together, my bond with them grows stronger. Seeing them again is one part of touring that I look forward to. Of course, it was this tour that brought me close to Rocky as well. Since he and I have been together, we have become friendly with other married skating couples such as Jenni Meno and Todd Sand, and Liz Punsalan and Jerod Swallow.

Years ago, everyone used to socialize and party on tour. Many people still do. As the tours get larger and busier, and I get older and perhaps more responsible, I tend to shy away from that scene. Morning comes far too soon on tour, and I don't need to face it with a hangover. Usually, the most I do after a show is talk to my friends for half an hour over a glass of juice. It calms me down. After a performance, I am hyper, and it would be impossible for me to go right to bed. However, an hour later, and I'm usually sound asleep.

That's not to say that I haven't done my share of partying. I recall one night, when I went out with some of the other skaters, I drank far too much and got very little sleep. It was stupid, because I had a luggage call at seven the next morning and a flight to catch at ten. I was so sick when I woke up, I could barely get out of bed. None of us who had partyed were feeling very well. We boarded the plane and as soon as I sat down, I felt nauseated. I couldn't get up to use the washroom because the flight crew was preparing for takeoff. I was in the middle seat between Lloyd and Alexander Zhulin, and Lloyd took one look at me and just shook his head. Although he had been out with us as well, he obviously wasn't feeling the same effects. I tried to be as inconspicuous as possible when I used the air-sickness bag, but it was so embarrassing. Luckily, I slept through the flight, but I woke up during the landing, only to be sick once more. Poor Lloyd. When he saw me reaching for another bag, he said, "Oh no, not again!"

Another time, Lloyd and I went out with the crew people. I was the only girl in the party, but I had a really good time. The next morning, half the guys missed their wake-up call. The ones who did make it to the rink couldn't believe that Lloyd and I showed up to skate. We both felt so bad that we curled up on top of the shipping crates, barely able to move. The crew people would walk by and ask us how we were ever going to skate. We had no idea.

When we were called for practice, Lloyd and I opened our eyes for a minute and looked at each other. He said, "I don't think so."

"We'll practice in our dreams," I replied. Then we both went back to sleep.

Just before curtain time, Lloyd began moving around. Because he hadn't eaten all day, he decided he was hungry. Although I advised against it, he went off to gobble down two cheeseburgers. For some reason, we were performing two numbers in a row that night. After our second performance, Lloyd literally ran off the ice, and I was too tired to help him. It had been all I could do to hold myself together while he was spinning and throwing me around the arena. I don't know how either of us made it through those performances. If we ever deserved a standing ovation, it was on that night.

Lloyd

Touring is synonymous with partying. It is not always the same people going out on the same night. Because there are so many of us, we often hit different nights. I don't partake in the socializing nearly as much as I used to, but there are usually one or two nights on tour that I live to regret the following morning. On those days, I may be very hungover, but I still have to go out and perform. That's the motto of the entertainment world: The Show Must Go On. I figure

I have done it to myself, so I live with it. Many times, when I have felt absolutely at my worst, I have been surprised by how well I've actually performed.

One night, Isabelle and I went out with the crew in East St. Louis, where the bars don't shut down until very late. We had such a good time that we didn't leave until six-thirty in the morning. The crew had to be up at eight, and were betting that Isabelle and I wouldn't be able to skate that night. It's true that Isabelle and I felt ghastly. We both fell asleep on the crates that hold the equipment and we couldn't even practice.

Just before our performance, I decided to have something to eat. Isabelle advised against it and told me to wait until after we skated, but I didn't listen. When we stepped on the ice for the first number, the lights shone down on us and I am sure my face was as white as the ice. While we skated, I felt so bad, I thought I was going to be sick right then and there. Somehow I made it through. But the ordeal wasn't over.

We were supposed to perform another number almost immediately. I got off the ice, had a drink of water, and went back on. The crew's face dropped to the floor as they saw us perform a second number and finish to a standing ovation. This time, however, as soon as I stepped off the ice, I was as sick as a dog. Isabelle just gave me one of her looks, and was probably thanking her lucky stars that I held it until after our performance.

When I haven't followed Isabelle's advice, she isn't the type of person to flaunt an "I told you so" in my face. As I said, she may give me a look, but she rarely gets angry. Then again, she's had a few mishaps of her own. When that happens, I keep my mouth closed. For instance, I recall when a few of us went out in Detroit. Again, it was very late when we got back to the hotel. We had an early call, and the group of us, which included Nancy Kerrigan, Scott Davis, Isabelle, and our trainer, Eric Lang, was tired and hungover. Eric had been sick on the bus on the way to the airport, and Isabelle and Nancy were ashen.

After we boarded the airplane, we took our seats. I was near the window and Isabelle was in the middle. We were just preparing for takeoff when Isabelle turned to me and said she was going to be sick. I handed her the air-sickness bag and tried to concentrate on the scenery outside. She fell asleep and I was thinking, Oh god, I'm at the window and I can't get up and crawl over her. I wasn't feeling great myself, but I wasn't in near bad as shape as my partner.

Isabelle slept the entire trip. I watched as Nancy, Eric, and Scott made tracks to the washroom, and tried not to think about what they were doing. Then the plane began its descent and I thought, Good. We're almost there. Then I kept my fingers crossed, in the hopes that Isabelle would sleep through the landing. No sooner had I made the wish than Isabelle woke up, and in her most discreet manner, was sick again.

When we finally arrived at our destination, I couldn't wait to get off the plane. It wasn't that I wanted to get away from the others, but I was hungry. We made a quick stop at the airport McDonald's, which Isabelle and Nancy wanted no part of. With eyes closed, the two of them sat on the floor of the restaurant with their backs against the wall. People were walking by and looking at them, but neither of the girls cared.

Isabelle

Everyone gets along fairly well on tour, but we do have our fights now and then. It starts with being around each other so much. I know I snap at people and wonder later why I did it. People are also sharp with me, and those are the ones with whom I normally get along. But three months is a long time to be with the same people. We see the same faces day after day, and sometimes the slightest thing sets us off.

Most of us try to warn each other. Many times, someone will walk into the dressing room and grumble, "I'm in a bad mood. Don't anyone talk to me." You know then to back off and let them have some space. Some days, I feel as if I'm in a perfectly good mood, but then I suddenly become agitated over the smallest thing, such as someone's taking too long in front of the dressing-room mirror.

There is also jealousy and competition among some of the skaters. A few get upset over what order they are skating in a show or even who is sitting where in an airplane. Personally I don't care where Lloyd and I skate in the show, or if I am in first-class or coach while traveling. It makes no difference to me and I do my best to stay out of those petty complaints.

Another problem arises when skaters want to stay on the ice too long. One year, during the opening, Lloyd and I were announced after Surya Bonaly. All skaters are aware that when the next skater or team steps onto the ice, they are to move alongside the boards. In other words, we get out of each other's way. Throughout the tour, Surya was inconsistent about where she was finishing as Lloyd and I were coming out. One night she would stop at one end of the rink, and the next she would be in the middle. And wherever she finished, she wouldn't move back to the boards when Lloyd and I were skating. The situation was getting worse nightly. We would always have to adjust our skating pattern in order to avoid hitting her. No matter what we said, though, Surya wouldn't budge.

One night, she landed her jump, and again, stayed where she was. The announcer called our names, and still Surya didn't move. She was right in the middle of the rink, and our path. When Lloyd and I make our entrance, we are moving at a very fast clip. Surya saw us bearing down on her and moved slightly to the side, but this time Lloyd moved the same way and knocked her down. The crowd gasped in shock. However, my partner and I kept skating. Surya was in tears afterwards, and although I apologized, I hoped she had learned her lesson.

Lloyd

Not everyone gets along on tour, but I don't think that is any different than what takes place at the average nine-to-five job, where there will be some people you like and some you dislike. We don't have to be friends with everybody in order to work with them. The majority of skaters, however, are polite and respectful of one another. There

Isabelle, Elizabeth Punsalan, Rudy Galindo and Liz Manley
knitting backstage at 1998 Champions on Ice winter tour.

Lloyd on a break from golfing in B.C. with Kurt Browning,
Scott Hamilton and Garth (a friend of Kurt's).

Lu Chen, Mandy Woetzel, Rocky Marval, Isabelle, Ingo Steuer and Lloyd
on a day off during the 1998 Champions on Ice summer tour.

At a party at Brian Boitano's house in June, 1998.

(left)
Lloyd as a clown—1999 Stars on Ice.

(below)
Lloyd with Tara Lipinski—1999 Stars on Ice.

Isabelle (above right) as a clown at 1999 Stars on Ice. (above left, with Josée Chouinard)
(below) Lloyd and Isabelle in makeup for Voodoo number—1998 Halloween on Ice.

(left)
Lloyd and Isabelle performing.

(above right)
Lloyd and Isabelle in costume,
parodying Olympic gold medal
ice dancers in "Fun and Games"
at the 1998 Stars on Ice.

Lloyd and Isabelle strike a pose.

Lloyd and Isabelle on ice.

Lloyd and Isabelle as the Blues Brothers.

are some, however, who believe they are stars and evince a holier-than-thou attitude. The opposite also occurs on tour, in the form of skaters who are unbelievably humble. They never complain and always have smiles on their faces. Someone like Yuka Sato comes to mind, who is modest, friendly, and well liked by everyone.

One of the greatest problems we have on tour is the competitiveness among some of the skaters. It's one thing if they are arguing backstage; it is quite another when they take their rivalry to the ice, where someone could get hurt. The worst of the adversaries are the women singles skaters, who can sometimes turn a routine practice into a bumper derby. These practice sessions can be ugly to watch. However, as much as I hate to admit it, they can also be highly entertaining. In fact, I and some of the other guys on tour sometimes make a point of standing by the boards while the ladies practice. You never know what you might witness.

When skaters like Oksana Baiul, Nicole Bobeck, Surya Bonaly, Lu Chen, and Michelle Kwan step on the ice at the same time, mayhem often ensues. Each is trying to look better than the others. No matter that it is only a practice session, the way they behave sometimes, you would think they were at the World Championships. They yell at each other to get out of the way, and some skate as close to the others as they can. Others purposely get in someone else's path. They actually run into each other, and one or both of them will be knocked down. Then the screaming begins.

This rarely occurs between the women who have been skating professionally for some years. However, Oksana, who turned pro in 1994, is one of the worst. She tends to think she is queen of the ice, and that everyone should look out for her. Surya is really bad too, and attempts to stay on the ice as long as she can. Everyone is supposed to get thirty minutes, but Surya will still be on the ice when the next group of skaters, usually pairs or dance, come on for practice. She won't get off until someone from management yells at her over the microphone. Lu Chen is just as competitive. The two of them are out there until the very last second. I think they believe that whoever stays on the ice longest has some sort of edge over all the others. As I said, it can actually be quite entertaining to watch, but it can also be annoying for those waiting in line for ice time.

If Surya is still on the ice when we come out to practice, I will blast her. "Get off the ice now, or you'll be hit. This is pair ice. You've had your thirty minutes and now it's our turn." Her mother, who is always standing by the boards, will shout that her daughter needs more time. "Fine," I answer back. "Go get ice somewhere else." Her mother and I have had a couple of yelling matches over this issue. Surya is a good person, and I like her, but her mother can be difficult.

I'll never forget the night I actually did collide with Surya. We were in Buffalo and for weeks, she had been changing her pattern on the opening number. Because we are going from spotlight to blackout during the introduction, for a moment the skaters on the ice are blinded. Therefore, it is essential that we know where the others are, and that each skater stick to the same pattern. Otherwise, someone could get injured. I had been warning Surya to stay out of our way, but she paid no attention to me. This one night, Isabelle and I were coming around the end, getting ready for the spotlight to hit us in a certain place. We were traveling at a very high speed, when suddenly I saw Surya right in front of me. I could have stopped. At the very least, that would have ruined our performance; at worst, a fast stop put Isabelle and me at risk. Instead, I kept going and knocked Surya flat on the ice.

When we finished the opening, I found Surya crying backstage. As soon as her mother saw me, she began to shriek: "You ran into her on purpose. How could you do that?" I told her mother that they both had been cautioned for weeks about the dangers of changing Surya's pattern. Besides running her personal life, Surya's mother is also in charge of her skating. Then I informed her that if Surya did the same thing in the next show, I would knock her down again.

Another discipline that can be very explosive is ice dance, with many ice dancers displaying the poorest behavior imaginable while on the ice together. They will never get out of the way of one another. During one practice session, Oksana (Pasha) Grischuk and Evgeny Platov were on the ice with the brother/sister team Isabelle and Paul

Duchesnay. The teams were at opposite ends of the rink, but suddenly began skating towards each other. We all stopped what we were doing and watched, knowing that a major collision was about to occur. The four of them got closer and closer, and neither team was faltering. The impact was brutal. Paul sustained a concussion and had to have stitches to his face, where he had been kicked with a skate blade. Furthermore, he and his sister missed a couple of shows because of injuries. It was a miracle that none of the others were seriously hurt.

You never see this kind of antagonism among pairs skaters. We have long been taught that conduct like this inevitably results in injury. And usually, it will be to the woman. If you fall on your rear while doing a jump, who cares? But no one wants to crash from twelve feet in the air. If the man is holding the woman, and he catches an edge while trying to sidestep someone else, it's again the woman who is going to be hurt. Pairs respect the dangers of their discipline, and thus give one another lots of room.

There is no doubt that we get more churlish with each other the longer we are on the road. Some can grow to detest other members of the group because of their attitudes or behavior. Certain people can be very annoying and will aggravate even the most mild-mannered of the skaters. Often, we are in such confined areas, it can become claustrophobic at times. People get frustrated and let loose. Some people handle their anger better than others though.

When my own temper flares, it is usually because I am upset with myself, and I will release it on inanimate objects. For example, if I have missed something on the ice, I may come off and punch a wall or door. Once I smashed a wall so hard, I broke my hand. I've also been known to throw chairs and rip towel bars off the walls in the dressing rooms. Some people get nervous around me when I show that side of my personality. Others get worried. They think I'm going to lose my cool and hit Isabelle or another person. But those people don't know me very well. I would never physically take my anger out on anyone, especially Isabelle. The only person I am hurting is myself.

Isabelle

Lloyd and I always have one big argument on the tour and it usually happens during the last two weeks. We fight about stupid things, which culminate into our not speaking to each other at all. Usually these spats begin because Lloyd is intent on discussing the following season's skating schedule. He is ready to start booking us for shows and competitions, when all I want to do is go home and forget about skating altogether. I tell him to leave me alone and that I am not interested in listening to him, but sometimes he just won't let up. He pushes me and then I will say something that hurts his feelings. Before you know it, we're not speaking to each other.

Sometimes, when things get tense, some of the skaters play little tricks on each other just to lighten the atmosphere, and it would not be unusual to find shaving cream in your skates just before you put them on to perform. Although that's never happened to me, I did it to Kristi once. During the last show of the 1998 Champions on Ice tour, I walked into the dressing room to find every item from my cosmetic bag taped to the wall. Everything from mascara to toothbrush was on display! Another time, Nancy, Kristi, and I brought some pastries, emptied the filling, and carefully replaced it with shaving cream. Then we took the desserts to the rink and served them to the guys. I made sure Lloyd got the biggest one.

Lloyd

Prior to a show, there is the usual excitement backstage. Fifteen minutes before the curtain call, we are in our costumes for the opening number. Shipped together from the previous venue, the outfits have been steamed by a wardrobe person on the day of the show. Our makeup has also been applied, but many of us wait until the last few minutes before putting on our skates.

The venues, on average, are more than 80 percent sold for every performance. Tickets usually go fast for Champions on Ice, which presents some of the greatest skaters in the world. On the spring tour, an audience can expect to see all the Olympic and World champions, while on the winter tour, professionals such as Dorothy Hamill, Brian Boitano, Viktor Petrenko, Liz Manley, Tai Babalonia, Randy Gardner, Rudy Galindo, Jozef Sabovcik, and a host of other world-class skaters bring the building to life.

On the Tom Collins Tour, there are usually about fifteen thousand people in the audience. But the number of people in the stands has never concerned me. As long as they are enjoying our performances, you can be sure I'm having a good time as well. However, you can never predict how an audience will react to any given performance. Some years I have been in cities where Isabelle and I have skated to a standing ovation. The following year, we perform a similar number in the same city, and although we receive applause, the response is not quite the same. A Saturday-night crowd will sometimes react entirely different than the Sunday-afternoon audience. You just never know.

Isabelle

Half an hour before show time, I begin to get ready. I hate wearing makeup and always wait until the last minute to put it on. Stage makeup is very chafing to my skin and as soon as the show is over, I take a shower and remove it completely. Some skaters will leave their makeup on until they get back to the hotel. I don't know how they stand it.

Once my makeup is applied, I do my own hair and then put on my costume. We treat our costumes carefully, because we only have a couple with us on tour. Lloyd's and my outfits are usually made by Micheline Boyer, a designer who works out of Montreal. Micheline knows exactly what Lloyd and I want. Moreover, she is very quick. We can call and tell her we need a costume in two days. Once we let her know the color and type of material we have in mind, she makes the outfits and sends them to us wherever we are. Because we have already been fitted by her, she has our sizes down pat.

The costumes we wear on tour are not nearly as elaborate as those we used to wear when we competed as eligibles. Some of those outfits used to cost up to three thousand dollars for the two of us. Now we spend from three hundred to a thousand dollars depending on the type of costume. Our "Blues Brothers" suits were more expensive because Micheline wasn't able to make them. Instead, she sent us to a tailor, who was familiar with figure-skating clothes. Even though the individual outfits aren't as expensive as they used to be, it generally costs us more than it did in our amateur days. Back then, we only required two or three outfits a year. Now we need up to ten. Multiply that by two, and you can see how expensive it is. Every now and then, however, we get away with spending very little money on a particular outfit. Lloyd and I will go to a store and simply purchase something off the rack. We call these items of clothing "casual." Lloyd might find a T-shirt or a pair of pants that would be suitable, while I may get a sweater or a leather jacket. It all depends on the type of look we want to achieve.

Once in a while, something will happen to our costumes that is out of our control. The material rips, or a strap breaks, and we just have to make do. One night I was about to step on the ice, when the zipper on my costume broke. It ran down the length of my back. With my skin exposed and no way to hold up my top, I didn't see how I could skate. Someone grabbed a roll of black electrical tape, and in a few seconds my back was covered in the sticky substance. Luckily, it matched the color of my costume. Everyone assured me that no one would notice it, but when Lloyd and I were performing, I heard an audience member say, "Look, she has tape all over her body!"

All the costumes are left at the rink after the show. They are then thrown into a crate together and shipped to the next venue. And trust me, you don't want to stand too close to them when they are hanging on the rack. Sometimes the odor is absolutely overwhelming. Not everyone is as fussy as Lloyd and me about putting on a smelly costume. As soon as one of mine needs cleaning, I take it with me to the hotel and soak it in shampoo and soap.

It's not just the costumes that develop strange smells while we're on tour. Everything I take with me requires a strong cleaning as soon as I get home. Because we are changing in and out of our street clothes, and leaving them in the dressing rooms, they too absorb the odors. However, there isn't a lot we can do about it. When you're on the ice performing as hard as we do, people perspire. It's just part of the touring life.

Lloyd

Mishaps occur both on and off the ice. Most of them are not too serious. A costume or a skate blade can be repaired. However, when skaters gets injured, they can be off the tour in a blink of an eye. That's what happened to Isabelle and me in the winter of 1998.

We were skating on ice that was only 150 feet long by 50 feet wide. (Every so often, a producer puts seats on the ice in order to sell more tickets.) I don't like skating on such a small ice surface because it is not conducive to showing off our talent, and more important, it is dangerous for a team such as ours that performs risky elements at high speeds.

On this particular night, Isabelle got too close to the flowers that lined the edge of the rink. In order to stop my partner from hitting them, I yanked her away. That severe pulling in the middle of our number, coupled with her being in the wrong position, caused an injury to her back. As a result, we missed over half the tour. Furthermore, Isabelle was unable to train for six weeks, and we had to turn down future engagements. It took her ages to get over an injury that shouldn't have happened in the first place, and cost us a great deal.

I am not saying that it is wrong for producers to want to make more money. But since they demand the best possible skating from us, they ought to give us the best possible skating facility, and not chop out part of the ice to fill their own pockets. If a tour isn't earning enough because of the skaters' high salaries, have fewer skaters on the ticket. Situations like this don't just arise on Tom's tour; they occur on every tour, and it is a problem that I constantly complain about.

Isabelle

The ice was small that night. And at the end of our second number I did a little turn and was getting too close to the flowers. Lloyd, who had his arm around my waist, saw what was happening and pulled me away. However, because I was in the middle of the turn, my back was twisted. As soon as this occurred, I felt a burning sensation, which went away. I finished the number, took a shower, and didn't feel anything again until the next morning, when I awoke in intense pain.

We attempted to skate that evening, but there was no way I could make it through the number. I rested a few days, then I tried again. After performing, though, I had to take another day off. Eight shows passed and we skated in five of them. Each time I fought back tears of pain until our performance was over. As soon as I got off the ice, I would break down crying. We dropped one of our numbers and changed the remaining routine to make it easier on me, but nothing worked.

I was being very stubborn, insisting that I could still skate. In retrospect, I should have taken more time off when I first injured my back. If I had rested for two or three weeks, I probably would have recuperated much quicker.

On a tour like Tom's, there are many other skaters. We are only one act and our absence from the show wouldn't have made all that much difference. But because I continued to skate, I was off for two months. I couldn't even go to the gym to work on my legs or upper body. Five months later, there were still certain moves that I couldn't do. Performing even a single twist pulled my back in the wrong place, and we had to eliminate that element from the spring tour.

It took a lot of time to recover from that injury. However, I don't blame it on the small size of the ice. Lloyd and I skate for a living, and I believe it is up to us to adapt to the ice size. Normally, Lloyd can do anything with me on the ice, no matter how big the rink is. He throws me all over the place, and I stand up and smile afterwards. This particular injury was just a total fluke.

Lloyd

During the 1998 spring tour, we were compelled to miss another couple of shows because of an injury I sustained. Only this one didn't happen on the ice. I was playing soccer in the arena before a show when I sprained my ankle. It turned out to be a severe sprain and was still bothering me three months after the tour finished.

Because it happened close to the end of the tour, everyone thought it best that I take off the remaining three weeks. I wasn't about to do that. I am a workhorse and I love to perform. So I decided to take only one night off. The next day I thought I was ready to go. However, Isabelle refused to skate with me, saying that she was concerned about her safety and wanted to wait for at least another day.

At first I was upset with her. When she was injured the previous year, I left it up to her to decide when she was ready to skate. Now I felt that she owed me the same. Besides, I had friends in the audience and I wanted to perform for them. But Isabelle was adamant.

Isabelle

I wasn't angry with Lloyd when he hurt his ankle playing soccer. We can't stop living just because we skate. But I was concerned for my safety when he wanted to return to the ice sooner than I thought was appropriate. His foot was blue and was so swollen he could barely fit it into his boot. I am the one who is 10 feet up in the air if his ankle gives out on him. I am rarely afraid on the ice because I am confident that Lloyd is strong enough to save me if disaster strikes. When he has an injury of that nature, though, he could hurt me or himself. Why take the chance?

Lloyd was so angry when I refused to skate that he wouldn't speak to me for a couple of days. I think he was really upset with himself, though, in that he knew it was a stupid injury. He also realized that the owner of the tour was not impressed. It's one thing to get injured on the ice, but quite another when you are playing a game of soccer at the venue. Lloyd wanted to be tough and prove to everyone that he could skate. It was definitely a guy thing.

Lloyd

Performing in more than seventy cities on one tour can be exhausting. By the end, I think we are all ready to go home. After a period of time, however, I miss not being on the road, and always look forward to getting back out again.

Touring is a world unto itself. And even with all the minor irritations that occur when you are cut off from the rest of society, it's really about stepping onto the ice and performing. For someone like me, who'd rather be in front of an audience than almost anywhere else on earth, touring would be very hard to give up.

Isabelle

In my opinion, a man doesn't miss home or family the way a woman does. When I'm on the road, I think of my mother often. I just miss her so much. As much as the men on the tour love their own mothers, I don't believe I have ever heard any of them say they miss them. But I need that connection with my family.

If Rocky and I are on tour together, it helps me from being too homesick. It's nice to wake up with him, even if I am on the road. However, I still hate traveling and I still long to see my mother and brother. I don't think Lloyd, or even Rocky, truly understands how miserable I become.

By the end of a tour, I am a very grumpy, impatient person. I snap at Rocky or Lloyd at the drop of a hat, and cry for no reason. I just want to go home. And I promise you, the day I hang up my skates and all the touring is over, I will never travel again.

CHAPTER SEVEN

Stars on Ice

Lloyd

THERE IS NO OTHER SKATER quite like Scott Hamilton. He is entertaining, humorous, and amazingly gifted. Moreover, he is a pioneer in our sport. After Scott won the 1984 Olympic gold medal and retired from the amateur scene, he realized there was very little opportunity for the professional figure skater. Performing as the headliner in Ice Capades wasn't satisfying to this four-time World champion. He wanted something more. Always the innovator, Scott went to IMG with an idea. And in 1986, Stars on Ice was born.

The tour was a new concept in the figure skating world. For the first time, Olympic and World competitors, who had resigned their amateur status to skate professionally, would come together in a show likened to a theater production. However, there would be no chorus in this cast. Every member of the touring show would be a "star" in their own right.

Figure skating fans had long been complaining that when champion skaters turned professional, most of them seemed to disappear from the public eye. It was true. The sports media didn't cover the

Ice Follies and Ice Capades circuits, where some of the skaters were offered jobs. With limited options, other skaters turned to coaching, commentating, choreography, costume design, and judging—anything to keep them around the sport they loved. There were no structured competitions, television specials, or tours staged for the professional figure skater. In those days, the Tom Collins Tour was strictly for amateurs.

With Stars on Ice, Scott created a winning combination: professional skating rose to a new level of entertainment that was rich in opportunity for skaters; and fans were delighted to be able to continue following the careers of their favorite figure skaters. It was a phenomenal plan and it caught on like wildfire.

Isabelle

Stars on Ice, which began as a small tour for professional skaters, currently plays in more than sixty American cities from November to April. Then a Canadian version of the tour starts and hits ten major venues. That's where Lloyd and I come in.

Being allowed to skate in both Champions on Ice and Stars on Ice makes me feel special in a way. Not all skaters have a chance to do this, but when we signed a four-year contract with Tom Collins in 1994, Lloyd and I told him it was important that the Canadian public have a chance to see us skate. After all, the public had supported us throughout our amateur career, and when we turned professional, there were no tours in Canada, other than Stars on Ice. However, since the tour opens at the beginning of April, it would mean missing a few weeks of Champions on Ice. Tom realized how much skating in Canada meant to Lloyd and me, and gave us his blessing.

I don't prefer one tour over the other. Each has its advantages and disadvantages. Champions on Ice takes me away from home for a longer period of time, but since Lloyd and I are performing in only two numbers, the skating is easier. Stars on Ice is a great deal of work, because we are involved in most of the group numbers, but when I finish the tour, I feel more well-rounded as a skater and entertainer.

With a cast of only twelve skaters, Stars on Ice is a smaller show. On Tom's tours, there are often as many as twenty women in the dressing room, fighting for space; with Stars on Ice, there aren't usually more than five or six of us. Nevertheless, that much intimacy can sometimes generate its own set of problems. With so few of us on tour, everyone knows each other's business, whether you want them to or not.

Lloyd

There is a big difference between the two tours. Stars on Ice is a show where the skaters are expected to contribute to make the entire production better, while Champions on Ice is an individual skate. In the latter, we each go out and perform our own numbers, and many of the skaters don't seem to have pride in the show as an entity. They appear to care only about their own performances. Unfortunately, some skaters don't even do that. At times, I believe this attitude can reflect on the whole show.

With Stars on Ice, however, everyone is there for the betterment of the show. It is a collaboration among the skaters, and all the people who work behind the scenes. There is a smaller cast than Champions on Ice, and every skater performs two individual routines. Because we all work together on the group numbers, Stars on Ice is more of a company atmosphere, rather than just another skating show displaying individual talent.

Because of the interaction of the group as performers, I prefer this tour over Champions on Ice. Skating in the same numbers with Kristi Yamaguchi, Scott Hamilton, Kurt Browning, Jayne Torvill, Christopher Dean, Josée Chouinard, Katia Gordeeva, and Brian Orser is fun and interesting. Moreover, performing on the ice as a group forms a bond between us off the ice as well. Our common interest is to make the show as entertaining as possible. This connection makes the entire tour more enjoyable.

Isabelle

The American version of Stars on Ice begins rehearsal in September in Simsbury, Connecticut. The skaters work for three weeks, then they go their separate ways. A further two-week rehearsal is required in November in Lake Placid, before taking the show on the road. When the tour comes to Canada in April, Lloyd and I have only five days to learn the steps.

Some of the original cast members drop out of the show when it comes north of the border, and they are replaced with Canadian skaters. Others stay in the show for both countries. When those skaters arrive in Canada, they are obviously well rehearsed. That means the new cast members, such as Lloyd and me, have a lot of catching up to do.

A week before the show opens, we meet in Halifax, where we rehearse the group numbers under artistic director Sandra Bezic. Although Sandra is in charge of choreography, there are others who help develop ideas: Michael Seibert, Lea Ann Miller, Jayne Torvill, Christopher Dean, and Doug Ladret are all involved with Stars on Ice. Each of them makes a significant contribution to individual group numbers or the overall production of the show. Once Sandra has overseen the rehearsals, she doesn't tour with us. While Sandra is there, however, she is the boss. Hers may not be the only word, but it is definitely the last word.

All the steps for the group numbers require endless practice. Just when I think I have learned them, and try to perform them in the group, I'll take a step in the wrong direction. Suddenly, I have eleven people skating towards me. Unless they are all mistaken, which is unlikely, I have to go back and practice again, because it is up to the individual to go over his or her own personal steps.

The rehearsals are long and exhausting, often running from eight in the morning until ten at night. Both my brain and my feet get tired. I think the third day of rehearsals is the hardest. Everything I have learned up to that point somehow seems to get all mixed up. Sandra keeps pushing us, though. She tells Lloyd and me,

"Just learn one more step." It's always just one more, and it's tiring, but in the end it's worth it.

In the 1998 rehearsals, Lloyd and I had almost reached a breaking point. I was still recuperating from the back injury I had sustained on the Champions on Ice tour, and because we hadn't been able to train very much, we weren't in the best shape. There was just so much to learn, and everyone in the show, except for Josée Chouinard and us, had been touring with it for months. They all knew what they were doing and we didn't.

Worn out, Lloyd and I dropped onto two chairs that were at the side of the rink. I looked at Sandra and said, "I don't think we are going to make it. You're going to have to cut us out of one of the numbers." Sandra refused, stating that she had great trust in our ability. Instead, she allowed us to leave early that night and come in late the following morning. By having some time off, we felt more relaxed and were better able to learn the steps.

I find it very frustrating in the group if I lead the wrong way or don't perform a step correctly. The rest of the group will keep going, and I'll get irritated with myself. I don't want to look as though I don't know what I'm doing in front of the other skaters. Besides, the quicker you learn, the better you feel about yourself. No one enjoys feeling left out. Eventually I pick it all up. However, I'm not totally comfortable until I have performed everything correctly in the first show.

Lloyd

There are times during the rehearsals when we don't know if we're going to make it. Being on skates for ten or twelve hours, and having everything thrown at us at once, can make for a rough day. However, I think Isabelle has a harder time dealing with the routine than I do. About halfway through the week, she often gets very stressed and cries a little, wondering how we are ever going to be ready for the opening. She likes to learn through repetition, and wants to practice the same steps over and over again, which is time-consuming. I don't like to rehearse that way. I have a good memory and find that I only have to practice a step a couple of times before I have it mastered. But we help each other through it.

Although Sandra is in charge of the show, and teaches Isabelle and me most of the steps, I often turn to Doug Ladret for assistance. Doug and I trained together for years and I consider him a very good friend. After his partner, Christine (Tuffy) Hough, retired, Doug turned to the production side of ice shows and is a tremendous asset to the skaters. Because we consider him to be one of us, as opposed to management or even the choreographers, the skaters willingly take his advice.

Most of the company has been on the road with the show since November, and are, consequently, very tired. The choreographers are considerate of this fact, and won't ask them to be on the ice while the newcomers learn their steps. Once we have been taught, they call out the rest of the company for a full group rehearsal. The veterans of the tour and those who have just arrived work well together. The newcomers tend to be excited and a little hyper. Our enthusiasm helps to recharge their batteries, while their matter-of-fact attitude towards the show tones us down. We balance each other out.

Once Isabelle and I have become acquainted with most of the steps, and the rest of the company is on the ice for group rehearsal, I find learning the routine much easier. All we have to do from that point on is watch the others and follow them. This way, we pick up the overall routine much quicker than if we were all learning it for the first time. Feeding ourselves into an established routine, where the patterns are already set, is so much better than starting from scratch.

I don't want to make it sound as if any of this is a breeze. It definitely is not. We still have to learn more than a thousand steps that are technically demanding. The 1998 Stars on Ice was the most difficult of all. Every number was more powerful and innovative than I had ever experienced before. The show required a ton of ability from every skater on the ice. I loved it. Mastering a show like this challenges my level of talent and creativity.

Since there are other new people learning the steps, Isabelle and I are not on the ice for the entire rehearsal. However, we are expected to be at the rink all day. Besides the group rehearsals, there are costume fittings, listening and becoming familiar with the music we will be skating to, learning the timing of the routines, or practicing our own numbers off the ice.

By the time we join the Stars on Ice tour, Isabelle and I are usually in pretty good physical shape. We've been through our training in the fall, participated in various competitions and shows, and then toured with Champions on Ice. Furthermore, we have usually prepared a new number for Stars on Ice, which we will repeat on Tom's spring tour. The second routine will be one that was performed on Tom's winter tour. Because no Canadian audience will have seen either, both will be fresh for Stars on Ice.

Before presenting a new number to an audience, I am always anxious. We have worked hard to put the routine together, but we never know how the audience will react. For example, the first time we debuted "Ballroom Blitz" was at the 1998 opening for Stars on Ice. As usual, Isabelle and I were nervous about how the audience was going to respond to the piece. Not only was the number new, we were performing it in front of a home audience, whose approval means everything to us.

When we finished the fast-paced number, I smiled as I heard the thunderous applause and saw the crowd jump to their feet. There is nothing quite so satisfying. We went on to perform "Ballroom Blitz" to ten consecutive standing ovations across Canada.

Isabelle

We receive more standing ovations in Canada than anywhere else in the world. I used to think it was because we were better known here. But since we've toured in the United States for so long, American audiences are just as familiar with Brasseur and Eisler as their Canadian counterparts. I now believe that American audiences are more critical; they see a number they like and expect to view something similar the next time around. For instance, American audiences went wild over our "Lady and the Man" number when we first performed it.

The following year, we did something entirely different. Although the routine was packed with difficult tricks, we found the audience response wasn't as overwhelming. They probably wanted to see Lloyd dressed like a woman again.

There are certain crowds in the United States who don't respond like most audiences. They are polite and will clap for the skaters, but unlike the always lively fans in Canada, they can be very subdued in their reaction to a performance. The worst audiences are in Los Angeles. It doesn't matter if it is day, night, or a weekend. We could spit nickels out of our mouths and they wouldn't be impressed.

When we debut a number before a crowd, Lloyd and I are nervous beforehand. It is not easy for us to continually come up with new ideas. We wonder how the routine is going to be received by the public. Sometimes we put together a piece that we thought was good, but that doesn't work before an audience. Until we get the crowd reaction, we always worry.

Lloyd

The actual dress rehearsal takes place the day before the opening of the show. By that time, all of our costumes for the ensemble numbers have been expertly prepared by Jef Billings. A renowned designer, with a background in theater, Jef has done everything in his career from creating Michael Jackson's first pair of sequined socks to designing Nancy Kerrigan's wedding dress. In the 1997 show, there was one number in which Kristi Yamaguchi tossed a knit cap into the audience. (In Canada, the role was taken over by Josée Chouinard.) Jef hand-knit each of the seventy-five caps himself!

During the dress rehearsal, we go through the entire production. Individual and group numbers are put on the ice just as they would be in the show, with every detail checked out. Do we have enough time to make fast changes between numbers, and do the outfits work? If not, the costume people can be busily working into the night. Are the lighting and music correct? Because it is all preprogrammed, any glitches would mean reprogramming the entire production. The skaters would have to wait for the adapted version to be prepared before continuing with the dress rehearsal. It's a very long day. It is gratifying to note, though, that as long as I have been with Stars on Ice in Canada, there has never been a time when we have not been ready for opening night.

Isabelle

Backstage at Stars on Ice is crazy. Unlike Tom's tour, where the skaters read or make phone calls during the show, the Stars on Ice cast don't have the time. With each of us performing in so many numbers, backstage is humming.

I always do my own makeup and hair. However, with the number of quick changes we do, other than a different color bow or ribbon, my hairstyles don't vary much from number to number.

Although we have someone to assist us, I try to make sure that all the outfits I am supposed to wear are ready for the quick changes. In this show, we skate, get off the ice, hastily change our costumes, and return to the ice within a few minutes. The process is repeated several times over during the show, and disaster can strike if even the slightest detail is overlooked.

One year, I had just finished a quick change into a sleeveless dress that fastened around the neck with three hooks. Lloyd and I were on the ice, and were performing one of our moves called fly high–say bye. As I was coming down for the landing, I felt my costume pop open. Apparently the woman who had helped dress me hadn't fastened the hooks tightly. The next thing I knew, my dress dropped down to my waist. And I wasn't wearing anything underneath! We were at the far end of the ice, and I'm sure the audience received an eyeful.

In a state of shock, I picked up the top of my costume and held it in front of me. Then I just stood there. We still had one more element to perform, and because Lloyd didn't know why I was motionless, he yelled, "Keep going." But I wasn't going anywhere. My dress wasn't holding itself up. Finally Lloyd caught on, and not knowing what else to do, we both danced a little.

Brian Orser was next to perform, and was sent out earlier than

usual. He didn't know why we were just standing there, so he casu-
ally skated down the length of the ice to where we stood, and gave us
a questioning look. Of course, the audience was as curious as he was.
It was one of the most embarrassing moments.

Lloyd

Backstage, everyone has different ways of warming up prior to the
show. Some people skip rope. Others stretch. Lately, I play soccer.
About half an hour before I have to get ready, I go out back of the
venue along with Shae-Lynn Bourne and Stephen Cousins, who
first got me interested in the game. The three of us kick the ball
around and have a great time. It really gets my blood moving. Often
we become so engrossed in our game when the production manager
yells, "Half hour," we continue to play for another fifteen minutes.
It doesn't leave much time to get ready, but the fun we have is worth
it. Sometimes we play indoors, and I think on the 1998 tour we lost
seven balls to the rafters or heating ducts. We'd be out the next day
to buy another ball, only to lose it along with the others.

When I come in from our soccer game, the first thing I do is
make sure all my outfits are ready for the quick changes. Although
the wardrobe person has laid everything out, I still like to double-
check. The thought of not having part of an outfit there, when I
have to be back on the ice in two minutes, makes me nervous.

After I am confident that my costumes are in order, I apply my
makeup, which only takes a couple of minutes. All of the skaters
wear a base of pancake or show makeup. Otherwise we would look
pale under the bright lights. Most of us have been taught by an
expert on how much to apply. Too little and we look sick; too much
and we appear garish. Then it's into the costume and skates.

Once the show actually begins, there isn't a moment's rest until it
ends. If we are not on the ice performing, we are backstage getting
in or out of costumes. The activity and atmosphere are reminiscent
of the ice carnival shows I used to participate in as a child. It's as
exciting for me now as it was back then.

Isabelle

Halifax is a great city for an opening. The audience realizes it is the first time we are appearing together in this version of the show, and seem to be as excited as we are. Furthermore, Halifax loves figure skating. The city's passion for the sport inspires us to do an even better job. That, coupled with our own anticipation, makes for an electric evening.

Lloyd

If I had a choice to make people laugh or cry during a performance, I would definitely choose the former. When I pay to be entertained, I am usually trying to take a break from reality, and I believe most people feel the same way. There is enough sadness in our everyday lives. I have been told that I have a flair for making people laugh, which I take as a great compliment. If I can put a smile on one person's face, I'm happy. That's why I love the comedic roles in our routines.

One of my favorites from the Stars on Ice tour is the spaghetti-western number we performed as a group in 1997. Scott Hamilton played a cowboy, and I was outfitted as a saloon girl who wanted Scott desperately. When I absorb myself into a character like this, I forget who Lloyd Eisler is. I put aside my own personality and become the individual I'm playing. I study the role beforehand, and try to think of ways to make it more comical. However, in a number such as this, the mere sight of someone my size, dressed up like a woman, and chasing after Scotty is hysterical in its own right.

Isabelle

While we are rehearsing these type of numbers, everyone is cracking up. Although I'm used to seeing Lloyd dressed as a woman, the sight still gets to me. Watching him strut across the ice wearing a wig, skirt, and lots of makeup is so funny. Then to see him chase after Scott, who is dressed like a little cowboy, makes us all laugh so hard, we have tears in our eyes. Even during for the shows, more than once, the skaters have had a difficult time keeping straight faces when we are standing before an audience together.

My favorite group number from Stars on Ice is one we presented in 1998. It was called "Fun and Games," and was a parody of the Olympics. Under normal circumstances, the Olympics Games are serious business, but in this number, the skaters made fun of every aspect of the competition. We mocked the judges, parents, coaches, and the skaters in a series of comedic skits. Lloyd and I played the Russian ice dancers who had just won the Olympic gold medal.

I don't know if the audience realized that every move the skaters performed in "Fun and Games" was intended to imitate someone. However, I believe they immediately recognized that I was playing Pasha (Oksana Grischuk). She had become so famous at the Olympics through her dramatic displays, both on and off the ice, everyone knew who she was.

It was for this number that we had our most involved quick change. Lloyd and I had just finished performing "Fly," one of our own routines. We came off the ice and Shae-Lynn Bourne and Victor Kraatz stepped on to perform "Riverdance." In the four minutes that it took for Shae and Vic to go through their number, Lloyd and I had to get out of our "Fly" costumes, and don a series of outfits for the group number.

First we had to put on a "Samba" costume, which would be seen when we portrayed the ice dancers at the end of the routine. Over that was another outfit, then the tracksuits for the opening part of the number. It was nuts. Shae and Vic were also in the group number, but when they got off the ice, they only had to throw on long black robes and wigs before stepping back out. They were playing the judges.

Lloyd

I thought the "Fun and Games" number was brilliant. The entire routine was designed to make fun of the skating world, and was an example of the creative thinking behind Stars on Ice. It was something that had never been done before. In the beginning, however, I was averse to our participation in it. As pairs skaters, I didn't think we could pull off a dance spoof. The more we submerged ourselves in the role, however, the more comfortable I was with it.

Another number that received a great response was the "Red Hat" routine. Created and choreographed by Christopher Dean, it was an extremely complicated piece, which involved all the skaters, and centered on a red top hat. With a piano set at center ice, and the skaters dressed in red, white, and black, we began a series of moves in which each of the skaters attempts to take the hat from one another without dropping it.

When we first began rehearsing this number, it was very stressful on the skaters who were new to the tour. The moves appeared to be so intricate, and we wondered how we could get by without dropping the hat. Any skater who has worked with a prop will tell you how difficult it is. Not only do you have to remember the steps involved, but now you are dealing with a piece of apparatus that doesn't always perform the way you want it to.

It can be particularly trying for pairs skaters, who also have to worry about a partner. Isabelle and I have used various props over the years, and realize that anytime we bring one into our act, it increases the risk of error.

While the "Red Hat" number was one of the most difficult to learn, after a few practice sessions with the entire group, everyone began to relax, and we went on to skate it perfectly in Halifax.

After not dropping the hat in Montreal and Ottawa, the atmosphere during our future performances of the routine became a little tense. None of us wanted to be the one who dropped the hat. Performances of the number in Toronto, Hamilton, and Winnipeg were again picture perfect. Now, we were all on edge, and things continued in this vein for the rest of the venues. It had become almost like a competition among us. The singles skaters hadn't dropped the hat, so the pairs can't drop it. By the time we finished the last show in Vancouver, we were all proud that the red hat had not touched the ice once.

Every year, the choreographers try to create something different for the group numbers. One of the most unusual entrances I have ever seen for the skaters occurred in the second half of the 1998 show. It was entitled "The Muse," and the skaters were dressed in black pants, shirts, hats, and sunglasses. As the music played, and the audience looked to the curtains for us to make our entrance, we appeared at the top of the stands instead. Entering from all directions, the small groups walked almost robotically down the aisles to the ice, all the while keeping time to the music. It was an extremely effective number.

Not every routine has appealed to me the way these numbers have. Every now and then, we have a real dud. For example, the group number that opened the show in 1997 was rather dull, in my opinion. We skated to slow, classical music, which isn't really Isabelle's and my forté. Although the number received fairly good reviews, it just didn't seem exciting or entertaining enough to me.

Isabelle

Because we play only ten cities in Canada, the traveling in Stars on Ice is much less arduous than in any other tour. We fly from city to city, and take buses from the airports to the hotels and venues.

Even our hotel stays are cut down on this tour. Because many of us are Canadian, when we play our hometowns, we stay in our own houses. For instance, when we are in Montreal, Lloyd stays at his house, while I sleep at my brother's place. In Toronto, Josée and Kurt stay at home, and when we play Ottawa, you'll find Brian at his own place. Staying in as many hotels as we do, skaters jump at the chance to sleep in their own beds for a few nights.

Show days are long for the skaters in Stars on Ice. Because of this, we sleep in as late as we want. Depending on where the venue is, the bus doesn't pick us up until between two and three in the afternoon. Until that time, the skaters relax. It's usually not a long drive to the rink, and we arrive by three-thirty. Then we head straight for practice, with each discipline allotted forty-five minutes on the ice.

Stars on Ice is sponsored by various companies. Therefore, when practice is over, some of the skaters meet with the sponsors for a quick dinner at the venue. This involves greeting about a hundred people in each city. We have dinner from six to six-thirty and then attend a brief reception, where we have our pictures taken with the sponsors and sign autographs. With the show starting at seven-thirty, we have to be backstage at least forty minutes early.

After the show, which is approximately two hours long, we shower, change, and then head to another reception. This function is held for a variety of people. Again, some of them are sponsors and their families, while others are individuals who are involved in either the show or the skating world.

I find it difficult to muster much enthusiasm for those gatherings every night. Sometimes I would like to unwind after a show by going straight to my room and reading for a while. The skaters don't have a choice though. Each one has to attend the reception for at least a half hour. If a skater doesn't show up, he or she has to have a very good reason, such as illness or injury. Like many skaters, I don't want to spend one minute more than I have to at the receptions, but I find that once I'm at the gathering, I usually have a good time, and am often the last one to leave. It's just getting there that I have a problem with.

Lloyd

I find the most demanding part of the Stars on Ice circuit to be the Montreal, Ottawa, Toronto, and Hamilton gig. With an additional show for a television taping in Toronto, we perform in five shows over a period of five days. That can be tough.

Because I trained in Kitchener, Ontario, for years and attended university in Hamilton, I have quite a few friends who live in the Toronto and Hamilton area, and since I live in Montreal, I know many people there as well. Many of them come to the show, and sometimes I find it difficult to give them the time they deserve. Because we have sponsors to meet, autographs to sign, and other public relations ventures that come with the territory, often I can do no more than say a quick hello to my friends. I'm fortunate, though, because they understand and respect what I do for a living. Hopefully, if I don't have a bus to catch, I will be able to spend more time with them once I complete my responsibilities to the show.

When my parents come to see me perform, it will usually be for the Hamilton show. Because the skaters stay in Toronto, we have to board a bus immediately following the post-show reception to return us to the hotel. This doesn't give me much time to visit with my parents, who I have often not seen in months. Hence, I try to talk to them as much as possible during the reception. I know it's not the best place for a visit, but sometimes it is the only place. However, not two seconds will go by without someone interrupting us to request an autograph.

I have absolutely no problem signing autographs. In fact, I am very flattered. Without the fans, I don't have a job. But if I am visiting with my parents, I will often ask the autograph seeker to please wait a couple of minutes. Most of the time people patiently comply. And two minutes later, I thank the person for waiting, explain who I was talking to, and sign the autograph. Every so often, however, someone gets very irate with me. They snarl out a few nasty words, then surprise me by still wanting my autograph. Because I am not afraid to speak my mind, I tell the party that until they change their attitude, I won't sign for them. Then I turn my back and go on to the next person. I believe in being honest. Furthermore, I think respect should be a two-way street.

Isabelle

The cast of Stars on Ice seems to get on very well with each other. I think that's because we are a smaller group. Although we may not all be best friends, we encourage and help each other out as best we can. I spend most of my free time with Josée Chouinard and Kristi Yamaguchi (when she is on the tour). We get along great, and spend hours together reading or doing embroidery. And we don't stop talking and laughing—or so we've been told.

Lloyd

There are always problems in any cast. When a group of different people come together for a long period of time, not everyone is going to see eye to eye. Certainly there are arguments between the skaters, especially during rehearsals, but the spats aren't usually serious and are soon resolved.

We don't have to be friends with one another; it isn't even necessary that we like each other. However, we do have to perform together every night and make the show look good. That, and respecting each other's talent, is our common bond.

Anyone with an attitude on this tour would be advised to leave it at the door. Every skater has earned a spot in Stars on Ice and is an integral and equal part of the show. If someone was unable to skate, it would create a big problem. Other skaters would have to pick up the pieces, and it would no doubt cause many headaches. However, since the group numbers don't focus on any particular skater, we all have to remember that we are only one of a twelve-member cast. If someone gets out of line, you can be sure that the others won't put up with it.

One thing I particularly enjoy about Stars on Ice is having the chance to work with pairs skaters Denis Petrov and Elena Bechke. For the past few years we have competed against each other head to head, with either of the two teams coming first or second. It's refreshing for me to skate *with* our biggest competitors for a change rather than against them. I also like working with Jayne Torvill and Christopher Dean. They have such a high level of professionalism, which causes the other skaters to strive for the same. Stephen Cousins, on the other hand, has got such a great sense of humor that he keeps everyone laughing. With someone as lighthearted as him on tour, it's difficult to take yourself too seriously.

Because we are all so busy during the season, we often don't have the opportunity to socialize with some of those with whom we have become friends. Kurt Browning, Scott Hamilton, and Doug Ladret are all guys I would love to see more of. Besides being good friends, we are also golfers, so whenever we are on tour together, most of our free days are spent at the golf course.

In the spring of 1997, I learned that Scott was pulling out of Stars on Ice because he had been diagnosed with testicular cancer. Of course, I was devastated with the news. However, I knew Scott well. He has overcome so much in his life, and wasn't one to lie back and feel sorry for himself. If anyone could wage a battle against this disease, and win, Scott could. And I was right. Scott was healthy and back on the ice in the late fall. Although he returned for the full American run of the 1998 Stars on Ice, he didn't participate in the Canadian version. I missed having him on tour. Aside from his abiding work ethic, he is just so much fun to be around.

Isabelle

Scott had participated in Stars on Ice in Canada. When he didn't do the tour in 1997, we all missed him very much. He is the type of person you like to have with you on the road. His happy and positive outlook on life is contagious, and makes everything we do together a pleasure. Without him on tour, I noticed a big difference; it was quieter and everyone seemed to be more serious.

Lloyd

We always have a party the night of the last show. Usually, the skaters meet at a bar, or if it is too late, we get on the bus and have our gathering there. The next day, we go our separate ways. Most of the skaters head home, but Isabelle and I leave for the East Coast, where we join up with the spring tour of Champions on Ice.

I always find it sad to take the last bow in Vancouver. It seems as if we have only just begun, when suddenly it's all over. In the three weeks we have been together, the cast of the show has developed an intimate rapport with one another on the ice. This is rare in our business. Skaters are used to competing and participating in shows or tours where no one really cares about anything except his or her own performance. With Stars on Ice, however, there is a feeling of teamwork and camaraderie. It's magical, and for me, it is difficult to let go.

CHAPTER EIGHT

Television Specials

Isabelle

WHEN LLOYD AND I aren't training, competing, or touring, we often appear in various television specials. Most of these shows are a collaboration between a network, a skater, and his or her agency, who then invites other guests to appear on the show. The formats for these specials are similar, and themes vary from Halloween and Christmas, to romance, depending on the time of year.

Unless a show isn't theme-orientated, which is unusual, Lloyd and I have to create two new numbers for each of the specials. For the most part, we know well in advance where we will be performing and what will be required of us. Notice is absolutely necessary, because we would never have the time to make up new numbers at the last minute.

Lloyd

Isabelle and I will do almost anything in skating we are asked. Although the visibility we get by appearing on a television show is great, taping an event for network television will not determine if we will accept the invitation. We go where the work is.

Unfortunately, there are not too many opportunities to perform in this type of show in Canada. Kurt Browning, Brian Orser, and Liz Manley hosted a few television specials in the past. However, it is something that isn't done here now. A television show takes considerable time, money, and effort, and Canadian TV doesn't appear to have the resources. Hence, most of the televised shows Isabelle and I currently appear in are produced in the United States.

Isabelle

One of my favorite television specials is Halloween on Ice, presented by Nancy Kerrigan and produced by her husband, Jerry Solomon and his company, PS Star Games. I like skating in the show and working with Nancy and Jerry. Besides being personal friends of mine, they are very concerned about the skaters' needs, and do their best to make us feel right at home.

The Halloween shows are almost like a mini-tour in that we skate in three or four shows in the Boston area, and tape one for television. Lloyd and I have participated in two of the specials, and both times we went out of our way to come up with innovative costumes and numbers. Most of the skaters do the same.

Lloyd and I tend to borrow some of our ideas for the Halloween shows from movies. One year, we did *Beetlejuice*, and Lloyd, in particular, really looked the part. The following year, we decided on *Casper*. Lloyd and I were both dressed in black, but I wore a white sheet over my head. For the non-televised shows, the effect was amazing. We skated under black lights, and when Lloyd lifted me in the air, the sheet appeared to be floating. For the TV version, bright light was required for the cameras, and the whole eerie effect was lost. In fact, I thought it looked stupid. Both Lloyd and I were disappointed about that.

For another number, we created a voodoo routine. Lloyd applied latex to his face, and we both used gelatin to distort our features.

The goal was to appear half-dead, and I think we accomplished that. I even scared myself when I looked in the mirror! The makeup was so effective that I used it on myself later for a Halloween party.

I love doing these shows. When Nancy and I are together on the Champions on Ice tour, we talk about ideas for costumes and music. All the skaters seem to enjoy them as much as I do. Because we have group and individual numbers, everyone gets involved and goes overboard with their costumes and makeup. The skaters get as excited as children, and in fact, the shows remind me of the carnival exhibitions I used to do when I was little.

Lloyd

Kristi Yamaguchi's Christmas specials are fun. Although many of the skaters who participate perform to traditional Christmas music, that isn't something Isabelle and I are usually going to do. It just wouldn't be interesting and enjoyable enough for us.

One year, we built a routine around the song "I Saw Mommy Kissing Santa Claus," and the audience seemed to love it. The costume I wore presented the front half of me as Santa Claus, and the other side as a regular man. Isabelle wore a one-piece sleeper set and carried a teddy bear. On the back end of her pajamas was a flap with the words, "Merry Christmas" printed on it. I'm sure she endeared herself to everyone in that costume.

Isabelle

We also participate in Todd Eldredge's Champagne on Ice, which has more of a cabaret theme. Todd has skated in our Dreams on Ice a few times, and is so talented at what he does. The American World champion is also a good golfing buddy of Lloyd's.

When we were practicing for the 1998 Champagne on Ice, Lloyd created quite a stir at the rink. He had put me up into a lift, and when I came down, he grabbed his ear. Apparently my partner had lost his earring, which was a large gold hoop. I stood on the ice in front of him and examined his clothes, thinking the earring might have attached itself to the material. But it wasn't there. Then we searched all over the ice. Everyone else stopped skating and helped us look for the earring. When we still couldn't find it, I told Lloyd that he must have lost it before we got on the ice. So a group of us went to the change room and began to search that area. We looked on the floor, in his skate bag, and among his street clothes. However, the earring seemed to have disappeared.

Lloyd was wearing a sweatshirt, a T-shirt, and a pair of leotards—his usual practice clothes. I asked him to take off his sweatshirt, which I shook out. Then I told him to feel over his T-shirt and leotard. Although I thought it unlikely, maybe the earring had slipped down his clothes. Well, Lloyd stood there and began to touch himself all over with everyone watching. Then he reached a certain part of his body, which I am sure you can imagine, and a strange look came over his face. "I found it!" he exclaimed.

We thought he was joking, and someone said, "No, Lloyd. That's the wrong jewelry you're feeling." Lloyd told us he was serious and tried to show us where the earring was.

"Can't you see it through the material?" he said. I couldn't believe it, and asked him how he hadn't felt the earring, considering the size of it and where it had lodged. Lloyd had no idea, but he went to the bathroom and retrieved his earring. We roared with laughter. None of us, however, could figure out how the hoop came off his ear, traveled down through his clothes, and settled in his pants in that particular spot.

Another type of televised show we do is the Symphony on Ice specials, where we skate to the music from a live orchestra. I enjoy performing in these shows. The music is amazing, and to have it played while we are skating is a sensational feeling. Normally, Lloyd and I don't perform to orchestra music, preferring rock and roll or something with a fast tempo. However, I believe performing to classical or orchestra music is good for us once in a while. It may not be the style we are known for, but it shows the softer and deeper side of us.

What is challenging about these shows is that the musicians are not always playing at the same speed we are skating. When we perform to a song on tape, we know exactly where to start, stop, and add the moves. With a live orchestra providing the music, there may be a few seconds between us and them, and those seconds can make a big difference for us on the ice. However, we are used to it now. We carefully listen to the music while we skate and adjust our performance accordingly.

Lloyd

Symphony on Ice can be difficult for a skater to do. Since the orchestra conductor never leads the music at the same speed we are skating in, we always have to adapt our performance to the musicians. We will create a program that is three minutes and five seconds. The next thing we know, the orchestra has speeded up, or perhaps we've slowed down, but somewhere we are apart by a few seconds. Since the musicians have their eye on the conductor, as opposed to the skaters' performances, it will be up to us to correct the timing.

As much as I am averse to skating to slow, classical music, I don't mind performing in Symphony on Ice shows, and actually find them challenging. Even if I didn't, I would agree to participate in the shows for Isabelle. She seems to like doing these types of numbers now and then. And when she's happy, I'm happy.

Isabelle

A few years ago, we took part in a different type of television special. It was called Blame It on the Blues, and starred Brian Orser, Shae-Lynn Bourne, Elvis Stojko, Victor Kraatz, and Lloyd and me. This form of television show requires the skaters to act. We are each given a role and perform it on skates. There is elaborate scenery and costumes and no live audience. Some of the scenes are taped at the rink and others are done at the television studios.

In Blame It on the Blues, there was one scene where Lloyd and I played a couple who were in love, and I was supposed to get angry with him. We were sitting at a small table that had a pitcher of water on it. My part was to knock the table over on Lloyd, take a ring off my finger, throw it at him, and leave. The scene ended with Lloyd running after me. The director made us do it over and over again. And I loved it. In real life, it is usually Lloyd throwing the furniture. Now *I* had my chance.

Lloyd

Isabelle certainly got into that role (Blame It on the Blues) and seemed to enjoy every minute of it. I wonder why. In that same special with Brian, one scene centered around Isabelle and I performing our usual pairs elements and acting at the same time. In it, we skated to music that had been selected by the producers. The piece was entitled "Insane Asylum," and Isabelle and I were supposed to be inmates in an asylum, who were trying to cope with insanity and the walls closing in around us. It was literally theater on ice.

When the producers came to us with the music and asked if we could skate to it, I immediately said yes. It was so different than what we were accustomed to. I knew it would spark our creativity, and I looked forward to building a number around this very strange music. We skated on small ice, dressed in straitjackets. Our makeup was pale and lifeless and, coupled with some excellent photography, the effect was very spooky. I would love to do more of these types of shows.

Most of these specials are produced and directed by non-skaters. Although many of the assistants and all the choreographers, such as Sandra Bezic and Uschi Keszler, would have skated at some time in their lives, the people in charge usually don't have firsthand knowledge of our sport. And it can drive me off the deep end.

The rehearsals for television shows are all different, depending on what we are shooting. However, most tend to be long, drawn-out affairs for the purpose of photography, rather than actual rehearsal.

If a shoot starts at 2:00 p.m., it is inevitable they will want you there at 10:00 a.m. I once asked someone why I had to be at the rink so early, since I wasn't needed until hours later. The response I received was, "Well, we just didn't want you to be late." They will put on our makeup at noon, and four hours later, we will be expected on the ice. Meanwhile, we sit in the greenroom and wait.

When we finally get on the ice, most of the time we just stand around for a very long time. Hours will pass, and still we haven't begun. The director will tell us it will only be another twenty minutes, and then three hours later, tell us it will be another twenty minutes. It gets cold and uncomfortable for the skaters. Although we are told to stay, I often leave the ice and head to the dressing room. My standing there would only lead to an argument.

Then there are the times when the director wants us to perform as soon as they are ready, without giving us a chance to warm up again. They think it is like acting, where an actor just has to say a line. But if Isabelle and I begin our performance without a proper warm-up, one or both of us are going to get injured. I get very angry in these situations and have often lost my cool. However, we go into these shoots as prepared as possible. We know it will probably be a hellish day, but it comes with the territory. The fun part is the actual skating. Sooner or later, we will get on the ice and do what we love to do best.

For all the television specials Isabelle and I have done, I have rarely watched our performances when they air. Isabelle does, however, and critiques our numbers and the overall production. I find it irrelevant. I have spent hours putting the routine together and then performing it. If I don't like what I see on television, there isn't anything I can do about it.

Other than the Olympics, I don't watch any figure skating on television. I'm on the ice all day long, and don't want to spend my free time sitting in front of a television set *watching* skating. Maybe after I have quit skating for a living, I will sit down and watch the tapes of our performances; in the meantime, I would rather be on the golf course.

CHAPTER NINE

Exhibitions & Special Events

Isabelle

E VERY SO OFTEN, Lloyd and I are invited to participate in certain events that aren't part of our normal routine. If we have the time, and depending on what we've been asked to do, we usually accept the invitation. Being involved in shows, exhibitions, and events that we don't do on a regular basis can be a refreshing change.

When we are not busy, one of my favorite events to participate in is a club show. These are little exhibitions put on by a skating club that feature the children who are learning the sport. If the club's budget allows, very often a popular skater will be asked to participate. Although we aren't paid near the amount we would usually get for an appearance, Lloyd and I strive to do as many club shows as we can.

Club shows are a lot of work for the skater. We perform in three or four shows over a weekend, and participate in numerous autograph signings, photo sessions, and receptions. However, Lloyd and I still love to perform in them. The audience is highly appreciative, the children are remarkable, and we are always well treated. Club shows are at the very grassroots of skating, and I have only fond memories of them from my own childhood. Furthermore, skating with children brings us back to reality, and reminds us both where we came from.

Lloyd

I think many clubs have difficulty imagining that skaters like Isabelle and me would be interested in doing their shows. However, they only have to ask. Performing in club shows is something we look forward to. Not only are they fun, but the environment in which they are staged is exactly where Isabelle and I came from. When I see a ten-year-old boy determined to make his jump, it reminds me of myself as a child.

Although we participate in up to four club shows a year, I wonder why we are not asked to do more. When we do skate in this kind of show, I am even more surprised when I hear that people from the community are curious about why we are skating in their town. From what I understand, many skaters turn down requests to skate in club shows, or expect exorbitant fees. This kind of response makes all of us look bad. Isabelle and I aren't interested in the money. When someone tells us they don't have much in their budget, we ask, "Well, how much can you afford?" We work from there. Our fees for club shows are extremely flexible, and we always do our own hometowns' shows for free.

I get such a big kick out of doing these exhibitions. Skating has been generous to me, and if I can give something back, then I'm all for it. Besides, Isabelle and I love to skate so much it doesn't matter where we go to do it. Whether we perform in a small rink in London, Ontario, or a 20,000-seat venue in London, England, makes no difference to us.

Isabelle

We have had many experiences over the years skating in outdoor shows. Because our performance can be hampered by weather conditions, I wasn't always keen on the idea, but we never used to turn down a show on that basis. We do now. In fact, since we last performed at the Cavalcade of Lights a few years ago, we refuse to do any more outdoor shows.

The Cavalcade of Lights is held in Toronto in late November. It is a night of festivities that centers around lighting a Christmas tree in front of City Hall. Part of the evening's program includes a skating show. The last time Lloyd and I performed there, it was cold and very windy. In fact, it was so blustery that in the middle of one of our lifts, which normally is taken around the ice, Lloyd was stopped by the wind halfway through.

For one of our numbers, all I wore was a little pair of shorts and a bustier. While I was skating, I was so cold that I began to cry, and in the middle of the performance, I whispered to Lloyd that I couldn't skate anymore. I was frozen. Somehow, we made it through that performance, but afterwards, we swore never to do another outdoor show again. The only way I would change my mind is if the event was meant to benefit a very special cause. Lloyd and I would have to invent a new number that would allow us to wear something warm—like a ski suit.

Lloyd

Trying to skate in cold-weather conditions is tough. We have done Cavalcade of Lights a few times in the past, and it seemed to get worse every year. The last time we skated in the show, it was thirty below, with very high winds. Although we were provided with full-length fur coats while we waited, nothing helped on the ice. Isabelle was so cold, she was crying before we finished the number. And skating in high winds was next to impossible. I had difficulty even turning on the ice. It was an excruciating experience and one we have tried to avoid repeating.

Isabelle

One year, Lloyd and I were asked to perform in a show on New Year's Day in Garmisch, Germany. Katarina Witt and other European skaters were going to be appearing with us, and we thought it may be interesting to celebrate New Year's in another country. Although Rocky wasn't skating in the show, he accompanied me, while Lloyd asked his then-girlfriend.

From the outset, we had a miserable time. Although we went out on New Year's Eve, we were surrounded with strangers, and I wasn't happy. None of us were. Everything seemed to go wrong, and our moods grew bleaker by the moment. Even the show wasn't all that great, and I couldn't wait to get home. Lloyd doesn't even remember skating in Garmisch. Perhaps he had such a bad time he just blocked it out.

Lloyd

The only time I remember skating in Garmisch was when we did the ISU tour after the 1991 Worlds were held in Munich. It wouldn't be the first time Isabelle and I disagreed. However, I will give her the benefit of the doubt. Perhaps I just consumed a little too much German beer, and it clouded my memory.

A show that would be impossible to forget was the one we did in Brazil in 1996. Organized by Jerry Solomon, it would take place in Saõ Paulo, a city that was not accustomed to figure skating shows. When we were asked to go, we eagerly accepted. Isabelle and I had been to Brazil for a vacation in 1988. It had been an enjoyable experience, and we were excited at the prospect of returning. Appearing with us on the billing were Nancy Kerrigan, Michael Weiss, Gary Beacom, Gia Gaudat, Rudy Galindo, and Calla and Rocky.

We left on a Monday and returned a week later. The plane ride seemed longer to me on this trip, and in fact, it was tedious. Being up in the air for ten hours at a time doesn't appeal to me at all, no matter where I'm going. Moreover, when I arrived at the venue and saw a little amphitheater with tank ice, I wasn't overly impressed. Because our elements are so big, skating on ice that small would mean extra practice to adjust our routines.

Once Isabelle and I got a feel for the ice, however, we had no problem. The show wasn't difficult to do and the crowd reaction to both our routines was great. For one of our numbers, we had decided to skate to "Copa Cabana," believing it would be appropriate for the Brazilian audience. And although they were very enthusiastic about our numbers, I found the response to the entire show to be a little strange. For certain performances, they were very quiet; for others, they went crazy, as if they were at a soccer match.

We didn't have much time for sightseeing, but I was able to get in a few rounds of golf. One of the organizers of the show was a member at a private club, and when he found out I liked to play the game, he invited me out. That was the best part of the trip for me.

Isabelle

We had been to Brazil before. In 1988, I was named all-around athlete of the year for the province of Quebec. My prize was a trip to South America, and I took my brother, his wife, and Lloyd with me. We had a wonderful time, and Lloyd and I were happy to be going back.

This trip wasn't the same, however. Nancy Kerrigan and her husband put it together, and it wasn't up to their usual high standard for planning events. I think the problems stemmed from the fact that they had to rely on local people for much of the scheduling, and so a lot of it was out of their control. But we did have fun. The owner of the rink took us out to a different restaurant every night, and from there we went to an assortment of Brazilian bars. I understand there is a lot of money in certain parts of the country, which is very apparent from the lush atmosphere at the many establishments we visited.

It was obvious from the moment we began rehearsals that the local organizers were unfamiliar with figure skating. Normally, Lloyd and I will not execute any elements in a rehearsal. The majority of skaters don't. We are often not warmed up properly, and performing different elements or jumps over and over again adds risk of injury. Instead, we do a walk-through. If a skater intends on performing a backflip, he will turn backwards, but just lift his arms in the air, rather than execute the flip. If he plans to do a triple Axel in his program, he will perform a little waltz jump instead.

When Lloyd and I rehearse, and the time comes where he is supposed to lift me, Lloyd simply raises his hand as I walk beside him. When we approach the part of the program where he spins me, he spins his finger in the air. Everyone associated with putting together a skating show is familiar with the various hand movements. However, it was clear the local organizers had no idea.

The South American producer of the show was sitting beside Jerry at the edge of the rink, watching Lloyd and I rehearse. When we were finished, he asked Jerry, "Is that their number?" Jerry told him it was. With a look of astonishment on his face, the producer exclaimed, "I am bringing these people all the way from North America to see that thing he does with the finger?" Jerry tried to hold back his laughter as he explained what Lloyd was doing.

Lloyd

I think every teenage girl in Canada is in love with Elvis Stojko. At least that's the impression I received when Isabelle and I were invited on his tour in 1996. I had seen the impact Elvis had on a Canadian audience when we skated together in Dreams on Ice and other shows. However, touring with him nightly and experiencing the crowd response reinforced my belief that this skater has enormous appeal to the female audience.

We have only participated in the Elvis Tour once, and that was against the wishes of our agency. Because Elvis isn't represented by IMG, and his tour was presented by Marco Entertainment (Magicworks) and the Landmark group, our agents weren't pleased that we had accepted his offer. Nevertheless, Isabelle and I wanted to do the tour. Elvis had appeared in our show, and we wanted to reciprocate.

Besides, we thought it would be fun. At that time, we didn't have an exclusivity agreement with IMG, so we agreed to do the tour. Unfortunately, it was our first and last. When our contract with IMG was next negotiated, you can be sure it included an exclusivity clause.

Playing in only eight cities, the tour was short in duration. There was a great cast of skaters, which included some outstanding Canadian athletes. Among them were Bourne and Kraatz, and Elizabeth Manley. Although the tour was still in its infancy, it went over big with audiences across the country.

The show was choreographed by Randy Gardner, who along with his partner, Tai Babaloni, had won the pairs division of the 1979 World Championships. I always thought Randy was very creative, but the problem was, we are totally opposite in the way we work. Consequently, we began to butt heads from day one of the rehearsals.

Randy wants the skaters to do the choreography every time he walks through it. Many skaters do require this type of instruction. But I don't. I would rather practice the moves a couple of times, then watch, finding it quite simple to remember. In my mind, the whole purpose of rehearsal is to learn the routines. As far as I was concerned, I had done my job. For those who couldn't learn as quickly—fine. Do whatever it takes. But Randy insisted I follow his orders. Of course, my back goes up whenever anybody insists I have to do anything. We argued, and the next thing I knew, Isabelle and I were being called into the tour manager's office.

When we walked into the room, Randy was already there, along with Michael Rosenberg and his coproducer, Elliott Kerr. I guess Randy had told Michael that either I had to leave the tour, or he would. We had a bit of a shouting match before settling down to a reasonable discussion. With Michael acting as the peacemaker, Randy eventually saw it my way. We went on to have a great tour, and I didn't miss a step.

Isabelle

The Elvis Tour was like a combination of Stars on Ice and Champions on Ice. There was an opening and a closing, a couple of basic group numbers, and individual performances by the skaters. It was a good tour, but we probably won't be doing it anymore because we do Stars on Ice in Canada. In fact, many Canadian skaters such as Shae-Lynn Bourne, Victor Kraatz, Brian Orser, Kurt Browning, and Josée Chouinard won't participate in future Elvis Tours, since they too are in Stars on Ice. Sometimes I think it would be nice to have an all-Canadian-member tour. With today's competition, however, and skaters working with different agencies, it would never happen. If we could go ahead and take part in future Elvis Tours, I believe Lloyd and I would jump at the chance again. We both think the world of Elvis Stojko and it's very enjoyable for us to perform in our own country.

When we skated on the tour, the thing that stands out in my mind is that we almost got kicked off. Randy Gardner was getting on Lloyd's case for the way he rehearsed. Randy is a very exacting person and would discuss at great length even the most basic elements. His perfectionism seemed to make the rehearsals last forever.

Lloyd, who doesn't like to repeat anything too many times over, grew impatient. After a while, he wouldn't listen to Randy. Then he ignored him. Randy would ask Lloyd to do something, and Lloyd would respond, "No. I am not doing it like that." Lloyd began showing up late for rehearsal, which was obviously intentional. Lloyd is well known for his punctuality. He is always professional and never late.

One day we were on the ice, and suddenly a stern voice yelled, "Lloyd and Isabelle—to the office immediately."

I was standing beside Rocky, who was on the tour with us. When he heard the announcement, he gave me a look. "I didn't do anything," I said, wondering why I was being called to the office. It was as if we had all gone back in time to our school days, and Lloyd and I were being called into the principal's office.

Sheepishly, Lloyd and I went to see Michael Rosenberg. Randy had obviously been pushed too far and had complained to the producers. I can't recall who said it, but one of the producers told us we had better smarten up or we would be sent home right away.

"Wait a minute," I cut in. "What did I do?"

"You are a part of it," was the reply. I guess everyone really does think of Lloyd and me as one entity. He mouths off, and I get in trouble. Although the story may sound comical now, it certainly wasn't at the time. The ironic part is, Randy went on to choreograph the Champions on Ice tours, and he and Lloyd got along just great.

Lloyd

In the later stages of our amateur career, and well after we turned professional, Isabelle and I represented the Beef Council of Canada in television commercials and print advertisement. We haven't endorsed many products over the years. Aside from Mondor Clothing, which is a skating line that we still design and endorse, the beef council was our longest relationship of this kind. It was also the first time we worked with advertising people.

Our initial meeting with the creative team of the ad agency occurred when we were called in for still photography. We spent six hours with ad executives and a photographer, who shot hundreds of pictures of Isabelle and me. When we saw the photograph they had decided to use, we couldn't believe it. It was a full shot of me throwing Isabelle up into the air. However, the only indication that I had a partner was the sight of Isabelle's legs at the top of the picture. Unfortunately, we had no control in what photograph they chose. We had been hired to do a job and that was the end of it. The advertisement ran in several Canadian magazines, and every time I saw it, I wondered why they had selected that photograph. It just didn't make any sense to me.

A while later, they wanted us for a television commercial, which was to be shot in Toronto. I was in the city, staying with some friends, and Isabelle drove down from Montreal with our then-choreographer Uschi Keszler. Isabelle had an important engagement the next day, but we were assured that we would be out of the rink by late afternoon. At 10:00 p.m. we were still taping, and in all, it took thirteen hours to film two thirty-second commercials. I was livid.

The waiting drove me crazy as usual. But this time I was more upset by the type of things they wanted Isabelle and me to do on the ice. These guys didn't have a clue. The creative geniuses had come up with all sorts of ideas, but hadn't checked to see if any of them could actually be done on a pair of skates. I lost my temper, yelled at the cameraman, and then smacked the glass at the top of the boards as hard as I could. Uschi, who had stayed with us to oversee the choreography, took me to one side in an attempt to calm me down.

It was very difficult for me to get back into the shooting. By then, I had reached the boiling point, and when that happens, I need to get away for a while. Because we had been there so long, however, and the clock was ticking away precious minutes, I had to step right back into the fray. The rest of the day was spent in heated arguments with the various people involved. Somehow, late that night, we finally managed to finish the shoot.

With all the fuss and headaches over the production of the commercials, I have to say, I was extremely pleased when I saw the finished products. They were excellent.

Isabelle

"There is nothing else like beef." If I said it once, I said it a hundred times on the day of the commercial shooting. It was a very long session, and Lloyd lost his temper. At one point, I thought he was going to put his hand right through the glass. No matter how tedious the experience was, however, we were bound by a contract. We stayed and did our job. As it turned out, I loved the commercials, so somebody must have known what they were doing.

I think it must be because Lloyd loves hamburgers so much, but we were also asked to do a series of French commercials for McDonald's restaurants in Quebec. They were run before and after the 1994 Olympics, and featured Lloyd and me answering questions from children at skating clubs, by remote control. We were filmed at many different locations in Norway and the children were in Quebec.

Because the producers wanted the commercials to be spontaneous, they didn't tell us what the questions would be. However, they were delightful. Both Lloyd and I smiled at the refreshing curiosity of the children, as they wanted to know if I was too heavy to lift, and whether I got dizzy up in the air. I thought Lloyd was fantastic, in that he understood and answered every question in French. The commercials went on to win an award.

We also used to endorse Sp-teri skates. Although Lloyd and I still wear this type of skate, the company recently took on younger athletes to advertise their product. That was fine with Lloyd and me. We realize they are trying to appeal to up-and-coming, competitive skaters.

The product we have endorsed the longest time is Mondor Clothing. I have worn their skating apparel since I was a child, and when they approached us, early in our career, we were eager to help out. Not only did they want Lloyd and me to advertise the clothes, they sought out ideas from us. In the beginning, we would tell them what we liked and disliked with respect to comfort, style, color, practicality, and overall appearance. After a while, we began working with the company on the actual design of the clothes. Designing is something I enjoy doing and may want to pursue after my skating career is over.

Mondor currently runs two different ads in various skating magazines. One is a photograph of me and Lloyd wearing their practice outfits, and the other is a picture of me and Tara Lipinski wearing the tights. How Tara got involved still amazes me.

Mondor had wondered if I could recommend a young skater for the ads. Long before Tara won the U.S. Nationals, I had met her and thought she was very cute and talented. Mondor negotiated with her and her agent, Michael Burg, and she agreed to work with us. We did the shooting for the ad in November 1996, and six months later Tara won the U.S. Nationals and the World Championships. The following year she claimed Olympic gold!

When Tara won the Nationals, Mondor called me and asked how I knew she would win. I answered them honestly. I didn't. It was all pure luck.

CHAPTER TEN

Living in
the Spotlight

Lloyd

BEING IN THE PUBLIC EYE most certainly has its advantages. Last-minute dinner reservations and theater tickets, and the best seats in the house are only a few of the perks that go hand in hand with being in the front end of the entertainment industry. But having a face that many people recognize also has its downside. Insignificant incidents will often get blown out of proportion, while stories of our lives, both on and off the ice, are frequently exaggerated.

Since I am a very private person, public exposure can sometimes be difficult. I don't like having to explain my actions, especially when they have been misrepresented. However, Isabelle and I have been lucky over the years. Because we lead relatively normal lives away from the rink, we don't generally receive negative press. I'm sure some of our counterparts wish they could say the same.

There have been several figure skaters whose irresponsible behaviour has fed the tabloids and gossip columns. The most infamous was Tonya Harding. In fact, the story of her involvement with the attack on Nancy Kerrigan probably led to the keen interest the public have in skaters today. Olympic gold medalist Oksana Baiul was in the news for several weeks after she crashed her car while driving under the influence, as was Nicole Bobeck when she was charged with home invasion. In most of these cases, I think the skaters were let off a little too lightly. They may have captured the media's attention because they were celebrities, but because of this status, they were probably treated more leniently than the average citizen. I think that is a disgrace. I don't care who you are: someone who breaks the law should have to pay for it.

An exception to this slap-on-the-wrist punishment occurred when Gary Beacom had the book thrown at him for tax evasion. Gary, who is Canadian but made his residence in the United States, decided he was paying too many taxes. Having the unique personality Gary does, the popular professional skater went to court to fight his case. Unfortunately, he lost and is currently serving time in a U.S. state penitentiary. I have known Gary for years, and the intensity of his battle didn't surprise me. He believed in what he was doing, and was willing to risk everything to stand up for his belief. Although I would not fight that particular battle, or follow the same path he did, I admire people who take a firm stand and won't back down from their principles.

Isabelle

I didn't know Gary as well as Lloyd did. They competed on the national team together back in the early eighties. It surprised me that he thought he could get away with not paying taxes. However, Gary doesn't think like the majority of people do. He was never one to follow the rules, either on or off the ice. Although the American judicial system gave him every opportunity to pay and get off without a jail sentence, he believed he was right and refused their offers. He even went so far as to fire his advisers and represent himself in court, a move that could have been his downfall.

There was a story going around among the skaters that Gary asked himself a question while he was on the witness stand. Apparently, it was so long and elaborate that by the time he tried to answer his own question, he couldn't remember what he had asked! I can't confirm the story, but it sounds like something Gary would do.

Gary's predicament would never have made the news, had he not been a celebrity. Because he is a skater, everyone knew what was going on in his personal life. That can be tough on some people. I know it was very painful for Brian Orser to have to answer questions when a story broke about his private life in December 1998. Brian is a kind and thoughtful man who works very hard to entertain an audience. Why his sexual preference, or mine, for that matter, should make any difference to anyone, I will never understand.

I feel very strongly about this issue and don't believe the public is entitled to know every detail about us. It's one thing if I want to tell you. Then I will tell my story in a book or contact a journalist. It's quite another matter when something intensely personal is dug up and dragged into the open. If I asked people in the audience how much money they made, or if they were having marital problems, I am sure they would be offended. I just wish people would realize that we feel the same way about our privacy.

Lloyd

I've had the opportunity to meet many famous people because I skate for a living. However, their celebrity status seldom impresses me. I may appreciate what they have accomplished, but their fame is of no consequence to me. I admire many people from all walks of life. The person who holds down two jobs to ensure his or her family's well-being gains as much admiration from me as last year's Olympic gold medal winner.

Having said that, there are a few people that I have been excited about meeting. For example, I enjoy the acquaintances I have made with various professional golfers. Because I love the game so much, I participate in as many tournaments as time will allow. For the last several years, I have been playing at the same event as golf-great Fred Couples, and I find him particularly interesting to talk with.

I also liked meeting Bobby Orr. Hockey is another passion of mine, and in my opinion there are few people who played the game as well as he did. When we were introduced, the first thing Bobby said to me was, "Oh, yeah. You're that guy who dresses up like a woman." While some people may not have been happy to be remembered for dressing in drag, I was very flattered. And although I am not an autograph seeker, I was thrilled to receive a well-known print of him playing the game, which he had signed and sent to me.

Isabelle

We are often invited to events that we probably wouldn't be asked to if it wasn't for our skating. Unfortunately, golf tournaments seem to be high on the list. Because my partner loves the game so much, he is always eager to attend. Once in a while, I will go with him. But I won't play.

Many people would enjoy the various functions we are invited to. But because there are so many, often I welcome a quiet night at home. Being in my own house is relaxing, and sometimes more appealing to me than attending a dinner or cocktail party. However, there was one event we were asked to that I was disappointed I couldn't attend. It was the opening of the Planet Hollywood restaurants in Toronto and Montreal. Lloyd appeared at the Montreal opening, and I was very upset that I couldn't be there.

Like Lloyd, I usually take meeting most celebrities in stride, but there are some people that I was very excited to talk to. When we competed at the 1994 Olympics, our exhibition number was skated to Bryan Adams's "There Will Never Be Another Tonight." After we returned to Montreal, a local radio station arranged for Lloyd and me to meet Bryan, who was performing in New York. When we spoke to him backstage after the concert, we were pleased to hear that he had watched the Olympics and enjoyed seeing us skate to his music.

While we were on the Tom Collins Tour in 1995, we were surprised with an introduction to Barry Manilow. Lloyd and I were performing to his popular song, "Copa Cabana," and Tom, who was a good friend of the singer's, thought we should meet him. We spoke to Barry for a short time before the show, and afterwards at the reception. He had liked our performance and spent some time asking us how we executed the various moves.

Lloyd has a good friend who lives in Idaho. Her name is Mary Poppin—just like the character from the movie (without the "s")—and she plays in bands. Through Mary, we met movie actor Bruce Willis, who also has a home in that state. Although it was only a quick hello, I got a kick out of meeting him. Apparently, he can often be seen sitting in with musicians at the local bars.

In the summer of 1995, Rocky took me to a Celine Dion concert in Philadelphia. Because Celine is from Quebec, and I admired her music, I thought it would be nice to meet her. So I took a chance and wrote a note to her agent. Then I gave it to one of the crew people, in the hopes it would find its way backstage. Within minutes, Celine's manager, Rene, who is also her husband, came into the audience and invited me and Rocky backstage for an introduction to the singer. She was very gracious and seemed genuinely happy to talk with us.

One of the funniest celebrity incidents that I can recall happened when we were introduced to actress Kathy Bates. Kristi Yamaguchi had just won the 1992 Olympic gold medal, and I was on tour with her. We had a free night and some of us went to see the movie *Misery*, which starred Kathy Bates. In the film, Kathy played an obsessed fan of the writer character James Caan was portraying. She held him captive in her house and actually broke his legs so he wouldn't escape. Kristi was particularly affected by the way Kathy said, "I am your number one fan." After the movie, Kristi couldn't stop worrying that something like that was going to happen to her now that she had won the Olympics. We began to tease her about her paranoia, and it soon became a standing joke among the skaters. Whenever she least expected it, one of us would look at Kristi and say, "I am your number one fan," and she would freak out.

A few weeks later, Kathy Bates came to see the show. At the reception afterwards, I presented myself to the actress, and told her the story about Kristi and how afraid she was since she had seen the movie. Then I asked Kathy if she would say the line to Kristi, just the way she had spoken it in the movie. Five minutes later, Kristi came into the room and was introduced to Kathy. The actress immediately took on the part of the obsessive fan, looked at Kristi, and in a sinister voice said, "I am your number one fan." Kristi was so shocked that she screamed. Some of the other skaters and I were laughing so hard that our sides hurt.

Although we joked with Kristi about having an obsessive fan, many of us know that it is no laughing matter. Occasionally, a person will get out of hand, and that can be frightening. Over the course of my own career, there have been two people who scared me.

Just after the 1988 Olympics, while I was still living in my parents' home, I received a phone call. The man on the other end of the line told me his name was Brasseur, and that he had a daughter named Isabelle, who was my age. He explained that his wife had left him eighteen years ago, and had taken his baby daughter with her. Now he was searching for his child, and wondered if I might be her. His question seemed legitimate enough, so I explained that my own father's name was Brasseur, and that I couldn't possibly be the person he was seeking. To reinforce my point, I asked what his ex-wife's maiden name was, and he seemed satisfied when I assured him that she wasn't my mother.

Four years later, I was living in my own apartment. I had just returned from the Olympics in Albertville, when I heard from the man a second time. He asked the same questions, and told me he believed I was his daughter. I explained again that it wasn't possible and hung up the phone.

Two more years passed, and in the exact pattern as his previous calls, he contacted me after the 1994 Olympics. Once again, he insisted I was his child. Now I was getting nervous. I asked, "Why is it that every time you see me on television, you think I'm your daughter?" He began rambling on with the same story, so I told him to stop calling me and slammed down the phone. Then I contacted the operator, who traced the number to a mental institution in Montreal.

After some thought, I called the hospital and spoke to a nurse, who was familiar with the man. She told me that he had been a patient for years, and that he honestly believed he was my father. After she explained the situation, I felt sorry for him, and told her that if it made him happy to tell people I was his daughter, to let him go ahead. But I asked her to please have him stop calling me. Because the patient hadn't listened to her before, the nurse thought it would be a good idea to notify the police and have an officer speak to him directly. I told her to do whatever she thought best. Shortly afterwards, I moved again and made certain my new phone number was unlisted.

Another time, when I was living in my apartment and skating in Boucherville, a young man began hanging around the rink. He showed up every day and watched the practices. Since the skaters and coaches were familiar with everyone who came in the arena on a regular basis, we wondered who he was.

One day, I came out of the building and he was standing outside. He told me that he was a police officer and invited me out for dinner. Although I declined, he gave me his phone number in case I changed my mind. The next day, he was back at the rink watching me practice. I ignored him and thought he would go away. However, he continued to show up regularly. I wasn't overly concerned then, believing him to be more of a nuisance than a menace. When he was at the rink, he wasn't doing anything to bother anyone, and since he was a policeman, no one wanted to throw him out.

One morning I walked in and found he had left me a big teddy bear and a note. A while later, I was performing in a show in Montreal, and there were balloons waiting for me backstage. He just wouldn't stop, and his constant attention was beginning to scare me. Lloyd wanted to talk with him, but the man never approached me when my partner was around.

I finally decided I'd had enough when I went to get in my car, which had been sitting outside my apartment overnight. There was a parking ticket on the windshield. I didn't have to look too far to see the policeman standing nearby, laughing. He said he had been driving around my area and just wanted to wish me good morning. I didn't answer him, and instead got in my car and left.

Now I was very frightened. He knew where I lived. If this had been anyone else, I would have called the police, but I wondered how I could ask them for help, when the man who was stalking me was a member of the police force. I considered getting my family or Lloyd involved, but decided to take matters into my own hands, and contacted him directly.

I told my "admirer" it wasn't right for him to be following me around, and that as a police officer he should know better. Furthermore, I admonished him for using his position to gain access to my address. As I spoke, I lost my fear, and in a strong voice I told him to leave me alone. My aggressive tactic must have worked, because I never heard from him again.

I haven't been bothered nearly as much as some of the other female figure skaters I know. I believe that having Lloyd at my side for much of the time has been a deterrent to anyone who may have been tempted.

Lloyd

In October 1996, Isabelle and I were inducted into the Sports Hall of Fame in Canada. According to the board of governors, through our achievements, my partner and I had brought distinction to Canada in our sport.

I felt greatly honored as I sat on the podium at the Royal York Hotel in Toronto. Being inducted at the same time as sports legends Robert Bedard, Ellen Burka, Ian Miller, and Guy Lafleur was enough to make my head spin. What I found equally difficult to believe was that we were being recognized just for doing something that we loved.

When Brian Orser, himself a member of the Sports Hall of Fame, inducted Isabelle and me, we joined the ranks of the country's top athletes from the past and present. It was a phenomenal moment, one I will never forget.

Isabelle and I have been presented with numerous medals and awards over the years. Among them was the Meritorious Service Award, given by the government of Canada. Although I was certainly honored to be recognized by my country, I wasn't exactly sure what the medal was supposed to represent. Apparently it used to be given to military personnel for service to country.

To be honest, I was slightly disappointed we hadn't received the Order of Canada, like some of our fellow figure skaters. To me, that was a medal everyone understood. However, I believe that aside from achievement, the Order of Canada is bestowed upon those who have been a role model in all aspects of their life. If that is indeed the case, I can understand why we were not given the award. Not everything I have said or done in the past could be considered exemplary, and unfortunately for Isabelle, I guess my forthright behavior is reflected upon her as well.

Isabelle

Lloyd and I received the Meritorious Service Award for achievement. It was presented to us in Quebec City by the governor-general, and I felt very honored. It wasn't a sports award, but was given to different people for various accomplishments. When I realized, however, that we were in the company of individuals who were considered heros because they had risked themselves to save a life, I felt out of place. Although I believed we had accomplished something good for the country, I thought that saving lives was more important than winning skating medals.

Being inducted into the Sports Hall of Fame was another matter altogether. That meant Lloyd and I had achieved the maximum in our sport. And it wasn't just figure skating, but all sports. To know that you are being recognized as one of the best athletes in the country is a pretty amazing feeling. What impressed me more was that we were being inducted along with people whom I considered to be legends.

From the time I was seven years old, Guy Lafleur had been a household name in the Brasseur family. He was nothing short of worshipped by us. My father loved to watch him play hockey for the Montreal Canadiens, and instilled that enjoyment in my brother and me. To be honored alongside someone who had been a family hero was astounding. I only wish my father had been there. He would have been so proud.

In early 1999, Lloyd and I learned that we had been elected to the Figure Skating Hall of Fame, along with Kurt Browning and Tom Collins. Aside from it being another strange coincidence that Kurt and I were named together (for years now, everything significant in our lives seems to happen at the same time, such as winning medals, buying houses, car accidents, even getting married), and although I was excited, it was not something I was expecting. I was certainly flattered, but I don't crave these awards. The simple things in life are more important to me.

Lloyd and I may be in total harmony on the ice, but in many respects we have entirely different attitudes and beliefs. My partner is forever setting big goals for himself, and thinks that I should do the same. But if I don't achieve anything else in life, other than having children and raising them properly, I would be satisfied.

Lloyd

I still have a difficult time believing there was a book written about our lives. When we were approached by author Lynda Prouse, who wanted to document our amateur career, I was excited to think that our story would become a part of written history.

Lynda, Isabelle, and I worked together for more than a year putting the book together, and in 1996 *To Catch a Dream* was released across Canada. It went on to become a bestseller. That there were so many people who wanted to know about Isabelle and me makes me feel very proud. That my children, and their children, will one day be able to read about my life is also a wonderful prospect. I feel very honored that we were able to have this. A book is forever.

Isabelle

To Catch a Dream sits on my library shelf at home. Sometimes I look at it and wonder how a book was written about my life; I always thought such books were written only about famous or important people, and I never considered myself either. However, writer Lynda Prouse did, and a year and a half after the project began the book was in stores and libraries across Canada.

We decided from the outset that we must be truthful. However, by doing so, we opened up our lives to the public. When someone tells me that they enjoyed reading about me, or they didn't know certain things about me until they read the book, it makes me feel a little vulnerable. I realize that people know more about me now than they ever did before.

My only regret is that the book wasn't translated into French. Because many of my family members don't speak English, they have been unable to read it. However, it has only been a couple of years since the book's release, and maybe it will be translated at some point in the future.

CHAPTER ELEVEN

Figure Skating – As We See It

Lloyd

I BELIEVE competitive figure skating at the eligible level goes in cycles, and currently Canada is at a low point on the international scale. This ebb and flow is natural and common to every country. In the mid-eighties, Canada and Germany dominated the women's singles discipline. Within a few years, however, the United States took over. Now Russia is coming on strong, and one of their women currently holds the world title. Why Canadian women haven't reclaimed their stance as contenders for world medals is anyone's guess. There is no question we have some very talented skaters. In my opinion, they seem to be lacking the fierce competitive drive that it takes to stand on the top of the international podium.

Canada has been strong in the men's division for years now. However, when Elvis Stojko retires, I don't see too many skaters behind him, other than Emanuel Sandhu. The same can be said for

Shae-Lynn Bourne and Victor Kraatz. As far as the pairs discipline goes, we have some good skaters, but I don't believe we have any great skaters.

So much has changed since I was competing at the amateur level. The biggest difference is the disappearance of a national team concept. When we used to head off to international competitions, there was an intense sense of solidarity among the members of the national team. In our minds, we were skating for the country, and each and every one of us supported and encouraged the others to do well. Skating for money and individual glory was never the issue. Our driving force was bringing home a gold medal to share with our fellow Canadians.

When Kurt, Josée, Isabelle, and I get together now to compete for a professional event, we still think of ourselves as a national team. As the sport has become more about earning big money, however, the focus is now on the individual. It has become a selfish business, where many skaters don't rely on each other to help them get to the top. Instead, they look to their agents and managers.

Isabelle

A country can produce only so many good athletes at one time. In pairs skating, Barb Underhill and Paul Martini were the team of the mid-eighties. Then there was a lull until Lloyd and I came on the scene. It takes a few years in between to develop the talent.

Currently I believe we have two good pairs teams in the eligible ranks. There is Kristy Sargeant and Kris Wirtz, and the newly paired David Pelletier and Jamie Salé. In 1998, Kris and Kristy ranked fifth in the world, and I believe they have the technical talent to do better. I also think that David and Jamie could go on to be world medal winners. In order to do this, however, I believe the two teams must push each other.

When Lloyd and I were competing at their level, we skated at the same rink with Jean-Michel Bombardier and his partner, Michelle Menzies. Lloyd and I had been on the world team for a while, but hadn't advanced to the top of the world podium. Jean-Michel and

Michelle were still striving to get on the world team. One day, we were all at the rink together for the first time in two months, because Lloyd and I had been away on tour. When we began to train, we noticed that Jean-Michel and Michelle wouldn't move as they normally would when we were coming around the ice. In other words, they weren't bowing down to the status Lloyd and I had obtained by competing at the world level. Lloyd got upset and confronted Jean-Michel.

"I don't know what your problem is," Lloyd said, "but because we've been away, you seem to think you are king of the hill. Well, you better move, or someone is going to get hurt."

Jean-Michel answered Lloyd very calmly, and I believe his remark changed all our lives: "I know you could be ten times better than you are, Lloyd Eisler. You and Isabelle have the potential to be world champions. I also know that we can be better and make the World team. I want you to be world champions, and what's more, I want us to be on the world team. For the rest of this season, I'm going to push you and I hope you are going to push us."

Lloyd and I knew that Jean-Michel was right in his thinking. In those days, everyone on the world team encouraged and helped each other. Even though Jean-Michel and Michelle weren't yet on the team, we used the same approach at our own rink. For the rest of the year, we pushed each other to become better skaters. At the end of the season, Jean-Michel and Michelle made the world team, and Lloyd and I became the world champions.

The drive to succeed is very important. Some skaters display a tremendous amount of talent when they are young, but they don't work it, and will never make it to the top of the sport. Another skater may have less talent, but a strong work ethic, and competitive drive will advance that individual through the ranks. However, no amount of ability or drive will help if the skater doesn't have the correct physical body requirements.

In all the disciplines, height and weight are key. I can look at a young pairs team and be amazed by their ability, but if the girl gains ten pounds or grows too tall as she goes through puberty, she may have a difficult time. If the boy doesn't grow to over five-seven, it is unlikely he will go on to be a World champion in pairs or dance. In figure skating, half the battle at any level is having the "right" look.

Even if the young skater has had the good fortune to grow to the proper height and weight, it doesn't end there. In a sport where body image is all important, skaters must keep in good physical shape. These demands can play havoc with the female figure skater. We wear skimpy outfits on the ice, and are constantly being judged. It's no wonder that eating disorders are prevalent in this sport.

I have never had a weight problem. In fact, I have a tendency to lose weight easily and sometimes have to remind myself to eat more. However, I see women in my sport who are constantly worrying about their weight. It's difficult to talk to them about it, because they won't always listen. They have it in their heads that they are fat. For instance, one year I was on tour with Kristi Yamaguchi and Josée Chouinard, who was concerned about her weight. She would see one of the other girls, who was very thin, eat an apple for the entire day, compare herself to the slim skater, and then say she was only going to have an apple for dinner. Kristi and I would repeatedly tell Josée she wasn't fat, and that her body size was perfect, but sometimes she didn't believe us.

Josée was sensible and strong, and fortunately never developed an eating disorder. You look at her now and see a beautiful, healthy woman. Others weren't so lucky. Too many woman in skating gain a couple of pounds and suddenly believe they are fat. They lose weight and feel better about themselves. So they think they should lose more weight, but it is never enough, and soon it can become a vicious circle. As their confidence drops, they don't skate as well. However, they blame their poor performance on their weight rather than their mind-set. Then they will try anything to keep their weight down.

Recently I was talking to a fourteen-year-old girl at the rink where I train. She asked me if I ever had a weight problem, and told me that she was worried because she had put on a few pounds. The weight she had gained was caused by normal growth; however, she was struggling with it already. I advised her against dieting, and told her to let her body take its natural course. Whatever the outcome, I explained, she must retain her health and confidence.

Lloyd

When Isabelle and I were competing as amateurs, there seemed to be more concentration on the actual pairs elements rather than the jumps. Originally, a pairs team had to execute a side-by-side double flip, then the rules called for a double Axel. Now triple jumps are mandatory. Because of this concentration on individual skills as jumpers, I fear pairs skills are suffering. The teams just don't have the time to work on them.

Jumping is not pairs skating, and if it was up to me, I would eliminate the side-by-side jumps from the technical program. In my opinion, this discipline should be about the lifts, twists, throws, spins, and death spirals. In fact, I would like to see a split triple twist mandatory, along with one other creative element, whether it be acrobatic or not. The beauty and strength of pairs skating is seeing two people working together to design one picture. With many of the current top teams, it appears as if the people comprising the pair are two single skaters on the ice together. The eye follows him or her, as opposed to the pair as a team. The throws and jumps may be superb, but the actual pairs elements are garbage.

Isabelle

I don't have anything against the teams executing triple jumps in the programs. Jumping was easier when Lloyd and I began, but after a few years, performing a double Axel was mandatory. Now the pairs teams have to do triples. I accept this as part of the evolution of the sport. However, I do believe that far too much emphasis is placed on jumping and not enough on the pairs elements. If a team is at an international competition now, and misses a jump in the technical program, the odds are they won't be standing on the podium.

I also don't understand why a triple twist isn't mandatory. Any senior pair should be able to execute that element. However, many people believe it is too difficult, and instead, they concentrate on the jumps. When I was competing, I had problems with throws, but I knew they were mandatory and worked hard on them. Pushing skating to the limit is what excellence in this sport is all about.

Lloyd

A couple of years ago, Isabelle, her brother, her mother and I, opened a skating rink and training facility in St. Jean-sur-Richelieu, Quebec. Although we are all equal partners, Isabelle's brother, Dominique runs the arena on a full-time basis.

Isabelle and I try to visit the rink in St. Jean, and help out the young skaters as much as we can. However, sometimes I wish I could do more. I believe I have a substantial body of knowledge to pass on, but unfortunately the Canadian Figure Skating Association isn't interested.

Although I have assisted some young skaters in the past, such as David Pelletier, it has not been in the capacity of official coach. In order to do that in Canada, I would have to go through a program, which is controlled by the CFSA. I have no confidence in the course, which is extremely complicated and outdated. Moreover, it was created by the elder statesmen in the coaching world, and mainly involves reading books. To the best of my knowledge, there is no requirement that the potential coach even know how to skate. In other words, anyone with the ability to read and pass tests can coach in Canada. Because the course is so long, it takes years to become accredited, which is all the better for the current coaching elite, who I believe created this method as an insurance policy to hold on to the jobs they have jealously guarded for years.

There are great skaters in this country who would make excellent coaches if given the chance. I am not saying I am one of them, but experience has to count for something, and I believe this should be accredited towards the program. I have a university degree in physical education, and almost thirty years' experience as a skater. Because I am so busy skating, I may not have the time to go through years of coaching programs, but I do know what it takes to become a world champion. According to the CFSA, however, I don't have enough knowledge to teach skating. No matter that I am in the sports and figure skating halls of fame. This is a ludicrous attitude, and one that is sending potentially great coaches to the United States, where such rules are non-existent.

I have voiced my opinion on this subject. More than once, I have argued my views with the president of the coaches' association, who at that time was Louis Stong. He turned a deaf ear, however, and actually became upset with me for not seeing their side of the issue.

I think the fault lies mainly with the CFSA. Once a skater leaves their realm, they don't want to hear our opinions. This is a shame. Whether it be as a full-fledged coach, or someone who is able to guide young skaters through the maze of the competitive world, experienced skaters could help the development of figure skating in Canada. We have so much to give, but are virtually being ignored.

Isabelle

No matter how much experience skaters have, they would still have to take the courses in order to coach in Canada. Since Lloyd and I own a rink now, I thought I might want to give lessons someday, and enrolled in Level One of the coaching program. After a few sessions, I wondered what I was doing there. Although I learned a couple of good teaching techniques, the subject material was very basic and lengthy. To date, I have only completed the first part of Level One. I just don't have the time.

I don't know why Canada makes it so difficult for people who have earned an Olympic or world medal to help younger athletes. We have so many experienced international competitors who want to give something back to their sport.

Because of the strict rules in Canada, I can teach only in the United States. Although I don't have the personality to be a full-time coach, because I would be too lenient with the children, I offer the occasional lesson. All that is required to coach in the United States on a full- or part-time level is a payment of approximately seventy-five dollars to cover insurance if anything happens on the ice. That is it. Coaches in the United States aren't required to take any courses. The American Figure Skating Association believes that it is up to the skater and his or her parents to decide if the coach is talented enough to teach. And I assure you, a five-time world medalist and two-time Olympic medalist would be a busy coach, because in the United States, experience counts.

I wish I could share my secrets with the young skaters in Canada and tell them how we made it. Making the novices aware of our struggles may help them put their own problems into perspective. Furthermore, listening to a veteran skater might motivate them to become future world champions.

CHAPTER TWELVE

Where Do We Go from Here?

Isabelle

THREE DAYS before the close of the 1998 Champions on Ice spring tour, I had what appeared to be a seizure. We were in a hotel in Chicago, and I was lying in bed with Rocky early in the morning. I had injured my rib the night before, and I complained to my husband that it was hurting so much that I felt sick to my stomach. That was all I remembered. The next thing I knew, I woke up to see Rocky standing over me in a panic.

I felt very strange. It was almost as if I was dreaming, or in another world. I was totally lost, and the terrified look on Rocky's face scared me. My poor husband thought I was having a heart attack and dying.

Apparently, Rocky, who'd had his back to me while we were lying down, heard me talking about my rib. When I became quiet, he assumed I must have fallen asleep. A minute passed, then I began breathing very loudly. Rocky turned over, and saw me experiencing what was later identified as a seizure.

When I regained consciousness, he rushed me to the hospital, which was across the street from the hotel. I stayed for two days while doctors ran a battery of tests. Nothing irregular showed up in my brain, and it was eventually concluded that I was epileptic.

This wasn't the first time I'd had an episode like this. In 1994, I was in a hospital for an MRI for my cracked rib. While I was there, I spoke to my doctor about having future surgery for a deviated septum. When he explained that the procedure would involve breaking my nose, I fainted. According to the physician, I had a seizure. When I came to, I explained that I hadn't eaten that morning, and that I had passed out because my blood sugar was probably low.

Fainting wasn't unfamiliar to me. When I was a child, I often lost consciousness, with low blood sugar always assumed to be the cause. After a quick test at the hospital, I was proven correct. My blood sugar was indeed low. Dismissing the notion that I'd had a seizure, I didn't follow up with any further medical attention and put the incident out of my mind.

Lloyd

I was still sleeping when Rocky called me from the hospital and told me that Isabelle had been admitted for tests. When he said that she had experienced a seizure, I threw on a tracksuit and raced across the street to the hospital.

For the next two days, I left the hospital once, and that was to have dinner. My only thoughts were of Isabelle and her health. I was worried sick about her and prayed that her seizure had not been caused by anything serious.

At that point, skating was way down on my list of priorities. In fact, I didn't even go to the rink. Seeing my best friend lying in a hospital bed, and not knowing what was wrong, well, I can't remember being so upset about something. I just wanted Isabelle to be well.

Isabelle

Lloyd stayed at the hospital with me and Rocky for almost the entire time I was there. I was admitted early Friday morning, and wasn't released until late Saturday night. After I was diagnosed with epilepsy, the three of us asked the doctors many questions, including what had caused it. We were told that the condition could be the result of an old injury. However, I found that explanation unreasonable. It was true that I had sustained various injuries over the years, but I had never fallen on my head.

At the time, all I could think about was whether I would be OK. The other realities about what having epilepsy might entail hadn't yet sunk in. The doctors believed that the chances of me having a seizure on the ice were slim. Therefore, against the wishes of both Rocky and Lloyd, I insisted on practicing for a short time after we left the hospital. I had been lying in bed for two days and I needed to move around.

The practice went well, and on Sunday morning I felt well and decided to skate in the show. Although I was ready, both Lloyd and Rocky had a problem with me skating. I assured them I would be fine. And I was. However, I can't say the same for the rest of the cast, who stood on the edge of the ice, almost as if they were expecting me to have a seizure at any moment.

After we left the tour, and I was back home, I made the rounds to a series of doctors. Once I knew what I was dealing with, I wanted to get as much information on my condition as possible. The only problem was, the more I learned, the more nervous I became about my future. I was warned that I shouldn't drive my car, sleep, swim, or even take a bath by myself. Then I was told that if I became pregnant and was on medication to control the epilepsy, my child could be born with mental disabilities. If I was to go off the medication, and had a seizure while I was pregnant, the fetus could be deprived of oxygen, and again faced the same risks. Every time, I came away from one of these consultations, I would be sobbing uncontrollably. It was as if the doctors were telling me that I might as well stop living my life.

I also had problems with the various medications I was pre-scribed. The first type was too strong, and made me dizzy when I tried to skate. The second wasn't strong enough, and I had another seizure. The last medication I was put on caused all kinds of side effects, including headaches and stomach pains.

Just before the second seizure occurred, which wasn't until the following October, I developed a pain in my knee. Lloyd and I were just about to get on the ice, and I began to limp. Since I hadn't injured myself, I wondered what was causing it. Although I had been told that pain often precedes epileptic seizures, I didn't link the two.

The following morning, I awoke with the same pain and then I felt sick to my stomach. Suddenly I realized I was about to have a seizure, and I was alone. With only seconds to spare, I lay down on the floor as I had been taught. Then I blacked out.

When I regained consciousness, I immediately called Lloyd, who came running from his room. Both he and Rocky had been instructed what to do in case I had a seizure. I was okay, but it took me three days to get back to normal. After a seizure, I feel disori-ented and weak. Furthermore, I lose my appetite.

After that incident, I decided I had better listen to the doctors for my own good. Although I had not driven my car since I had been di-agnosed, in the fear that I could hurt myself or someone else, I had continued to sleep alone while I was on the road. From then on, I made sure that if Rocky wasn't on tour with me, I had an adjoining room with one of the other women, and the door was always left ajar.

Lloyd

Once we had been told that Isabelle was epileptic, we realized that it was going to change our career. However, we had the entire summer to decide what we were going to do in the fall. Meanwhile, Isabelle was trying to get used to her medication. She didn't feel well and was always worried. I guess the doctors she had been seeing didn't have the greatest bedside manner, and Isabelle was very upset when they cautioned her about having children.

She was also fretting about whether we would be able to skate properly in the fall. My only answer to her was, "Who cares?" And I really meant it. For the first time in my life, skating didn't matter to me. I told her if she felt well enough to skate in September, we would play it by ear. Maybe we would have to step back and only appear at the odd show, or perhaps our programs could be adapted. If all else failed, we would quit. Putting her health in jeopardy wasn't an option I was willing to entertain.

Isabelle

I was so frightened. The medication I was on made me feel tired and I seemed to be emotional all the time. I didn't like depending on others so much, and often felt as if I was being baby-sat. Moreover, the thought of not having children was driving me crazy. I was getting more worried by the day.

Every doctor I saw couldn't explain my condition, and instead gave me endless lists of what I could and couldn't do. Some told me that since stress was often the cause, I had better relax more. Others said that I should get more sleep and that I had to ensure I was eating properly. I was getting fed up and decided that I wasn't going to live my life in a padded room just waiting for the next seizure. I skated and took reasonable caution with respect to my condition. Meanwhile, I continued to search for a doctor who could give me some answers I could accept.

I went to three different neurologists before I finally settled on one physician in Philadelphia. This doctor told me that although I had some signs of epilepsy, the other symptoms I was experiencing weren't related to the disorder. He put me through a series of examinations, including a sleep deprivation test, during which he ran an EEG of my brain. Again, the tests showed no indication that I had epilepsy. The more he saw me, the more he was convinced that I wasn't suffering from the disease. Finally, he suggested I see a cardiologist.

At this stage, willing to try anything, I went to the specialist, who put me through several more examinations. For the last test, I was strapped to a tilt table and lifted to a standing position. The doctor told me that if something was wrong with my heart, I would faint.

As the table slowly came to a vertical position, I felt like the monster in the Frankenstein movie. After a couple of seconds, I said, "Oh. I'm dizzy!" The doctor and nurse, who had stayed in the room, looked at me in concern. But I told them I was only joking. They went back to their machines and I just stood there tied to that table. I could hear my heartbeat on the monitor and wondered what I was going to say to them next.

After seven minutes, I began to feel light-headed, and called out to alert them, but I think they thought I was joking again. They checked my blood pressure, which was normal, and said there was no way I could be dizzy. As my vision blurred, I cried out, "I am very hot and now I feel sick to my stomach." The last thing I remember saying was, "That's it!" Then I fainted.

I was told later that when I passed out, my heart stopped beating, which was an indication of the condition I really had. They let sixteen seconds pass to see if I would convulse, which I did. However, I wasn't coming out it. The doctor quickly shot adrenaline into my body in an attempt to restart my heart, but still I continued to convulse. The adrenaline apparently had an adverse effect and made the convulsions worse. Twenty-five seconds had now passed, and the specialist wasn't prepared for anyone to be out that long. The nurse ran to find Valium, which they hoped would slow down the convulsions. When she came back with the drug, I was just coming out of the seizure. My heart had stopped beating for thirty-one seconds.

The doctors had only been using the tilt-table test for a few years. In that period, the quickest someone had fainted was after twenty minutes; and the longest time someone's heart had stopped beating was for twelve seconds. I had broken the records by a long shot.

When I came to, the doctor was patting my head, saying, "I am very sorry." I guess I had him frantic with worry. When he told me the diagnosis, however, I was so relieved that I could have hugged him. And I would have, if my arms hadn't been tied down to the table.

My condition is known as vasodepressor syncope, meaning that while I am at rest, my heart will start pumping too fast. It can be caused by any number of things including an injury, not enough sleep, alcohol, caffeine, or even someone telling me the gory details of an operation or a movie they have just seen. Normally, the heart pumps fast as a result of physical activity, and the blood vessels will open to allow more blood and oxygen to flow through the body. But because this happens to me when I am not engaged in a physical activity, my brain tells my heart to slow down. The message comes on a little too strong and my heart stops beating altogether. My blood pressure drops, I get dizzy, and I faint. If my heart stops for more than sixteen seconds, I go into convulsions.

Apparently this problem is not uncommon among young women. I have since been put on a medication to control my heart rate, and so far, I haven't had another fainting spell. But because my heart rate is maintained at the same level, and there isn't enough oxygen going through my body, my fingers and feet get numb when I am skating, and sometimes my legs get tired. Although I wonder if I will ever get used to it, at least I know that unless I get badly injured, I will never faint on the ice. As long as I am involved in a physical activity, my brain is never going to signal my heart to slow down.

The medication isn't foolproof. I could still faint, but now my heart probably won't stop beating for longer periods of time. Most important to me is knowing that I can have children. When I get pregnant, I will go off the medication and try hard not to provoke any fainting spells. If I pass out while I am not on the medication, I know now that my heart might stop beating, but they tell me it will start up again. And unless it doesn't stop for more than two minutes, it will not be life-threatening to me or my unborn child.

The doctors told me that some people with vasodepressor syncope will have a pacemaker installed, which is more reliable than the medication. Until I have finished skating, I don't think that would be a good option for me. Although they also informed me that I could go for further tests to determine why my heart stops beating for such a long period of time, it isn't something I wish to pursue now. I have had enough doctors and hospitals to last me a very long time.

Lloyd

Once Isabelle had been diagnosed properly, I noticed a huge change in her mood. Finally she knew exactly what was wrong with her and was able to deal with it. There may be some side effects from her medication, but they won't be as detrimental as having epilepsy. I think the biggest joy for her came when she realized there would be no problem in her having children. That was the most important issue for her.

However, I still watch her like a hawk while we are skating. I am always looking for signs to make sure she is okay, and we probably communicate more now than we ever did, if that's possible. If she gets the slightest bit dizzy, we slow down and take a break, or move something in the program to make it better for her. Many years ago, I promised Isabelle's father that I would always look after her. It is a vow I took very seriously and intend to keep.

Isabelle

I still miss my dad so much. Sometimes I see something that reminds me of him and I get very sad. When I was going through this frightening ordeal, I tried to speak to my father and ask him why this was happening to me. Lately, I have been having a harder time trying to find him. I think: Where are you? Why are you so far away? I just don't feel his presence as much as I used to.

Facing my illness caused me to reflect a great deal about my past and future. I always believed that family and friends were the most important thing on earth, and being ill only served to reinforce my belief. When I thought I might be unable to have a healthy child, it nearly killed me. Having children and passing on the values that my own parents taught me is something I yearn for.

Rocky and I have talked about starting a family within the next couple of years, but I don't think I am ready to give up skating yet. And if I had a child, I don't know whether I could continue a career that takes me away from home so much. I'm just not sure. Obviously Rocky and I will make the decision together.

I would also speak with Lloyd. A decision like this will change his life as well and I would never do anything to hurt our career. If I decided to skate and have a child, we would have to schedule when it would be best for me to become pregnant.

Lloyd

Isabelle and I have always compromised with respect to decisions that would affect our career. I have always known that she might want to end our partnership earlier than I would like. However, as in the past, we will sit down together and talk about it when the time comes.

We have already discussed her desire to have children. Whether she will want to continue to skate is something only she can decide. In the meantime, we now ensure that our contracts are shorter than they were in the past. As opposed to the four-year deals we used to make, we now don't sign anything that will take us past one, or two years, at the most. We are both willing to make a commitment to each other and our career for at least that amount of time. When these contracts expire, we will go from there. Obviously, if something happens before that time, we will just have to deal with it.

I think it is fairly obvious to anyone who knows us that it will probably be Isabelle who makes the final decision about when our skating career is finished. People have asked me if I would ever consider getting another partner if Isabelle wanted to stop skating before I did. My answer is always the same. When our career is over, my career is over. Isabelle and I have spent thirteen years together, and I don't think there is anyone who could replace what she has meant to me in both my personal and professional life.

Isabelle

There is no question that I want a life outside of skating. Some nights, when I am on tour, I wonder what I'm doing on the road. In fact, I have been asking myself that question a great deal lately. I watch and listen to my friends in the sport, and realize that skating is what they live for. They come home from touring and can't wait for the next season to begin. Until it does, the sport is always on their minds. When I go home, I don't think about skating at all.

One night, while I was on the 1999 Champions on Ice winter tour, I spoke to Dorothy Hamill. She told me that she stopped skating for many years, but eventually realized that stepping onto the ice was a passion for her. She was compelled to return to figure skating. As I sat listening to Dorothy, I suddenly realized that I have never felt that way about skating. I don't want to disappoint people by saying that, but it is the truth. Sometimes I don't know how I ended up in the skating world and actually went so far. If I had tried to pursue singles skating, I am certain I wouldn't have stayed in the sport very long. I am a follower. And because skating is Lloyd's passion—it's all he talks about day and night—he kept me going. His drive motivated me.

Maybe I am just mentally and physically tired. For so many years now, I had to summon up everything I had in order to follow Lloyd. He is so much stronger than I am. But it was not just Lloyd. Before him were my father and coaches. They were strong people as well, and pushed me to my limit. When I was skating amateur, I needed their strength in order to succeed. All of them have asked a lot from me, and without them, I would never have given so much of myself.

I like skating and I love to entertain, and if someone told me I had to give it all up tomorrow, I certainly would be sad. But I wouldn't be devastated. Although the sport has been great to me, I know I would be able to get on with my life.

Lloyd

My love for skating and continual drive to excel are what have kept me in this sport so long. I want to keep growing, and believe I can accomplish even more in my career. When the day comes that I am not quite as quick or entertaining as I used to be, then I will know it is time to go home. And I will do so with no regrets. One of the most important things to me is to retire while I am still at the top of my game.

However, I believe that won't be for a few years yet. For the 1998–99 season, Isabelle and I made up new elements and moves. Our programs are more creative than ever, and I believe we can do even more. Certainly our growth won't be in leaps and bounds. What we next develop may be small, but I guarantee people will notice.

Isabelle

For the first time in so many years, Lloyd and I won't be participating in the next Champions on Ice spring tour. We have done it for so long now, and I needed a break. Moreover, I haven't experienced springtime in ten years. People forget that we live in hotels, rinks, buses, and airplanes. We don't go outside to see the flowers blooming. I want to change that.

To wake up on a Saturday morning in my own bed and go outside on the patio to have breakfast with my husband is something I long for. Taking a leisurely stroll and chatting with neighbors may sound boring to someone who does it every day. But I crave that type of lifestyle. I am not talking about quitting skating, but I believe there has to be a happy medium.

I think this rest from touring will also be good for our skating. The time away from skating should rejuvenate our enthusiasm for the sport and help us to be even more creative in the new season.

Lloyd

I know Isabelle needed a break. In a way, I did too. When Isabelle got sick, it was a traumatic time for all of us. We didn't know what the future would hold on either a personal or professional level. I guess none of us ever really do, but somehow her illness made me look at things differently. Taking life and people for granted is something I try not to do now.

Sometimes I wonder where I will be in ten years and if I will be happy. Skating has taken up so much of my time that planning for the future is difficult. I like to think, however, that there is someone or something out there that will make me want to stay at home. Beyond knowing that I would like to have a family of my own, I am very uncertain what the future will bring for me. My personality wouldn't allow me to retire and do nothing. I would always have to stay busy, and more than likely, whatever new career path I choose, it will probably have something to do with sport. When you have loved your lifestyle as much as I have, it is hard to think of giving it up completely.

Isabelle

What I do in the future depends on how tired and burnt out I am after I finish skating. Right now, I like to think that in five years I will have one child and be planning for another. Perhaps Lloyd and I will still be skating, but if that is the case, it would be for special events and shows rather than tours. I can also envision owning a craft store. Crafting is something I have done for years, and I can't picture my future without it.

More than anything, I want to be at home with my family. Taking my children to hockey or ballet classes, picking them up from school, and helping them with their homework seems like the perfect life to me. What may be ordinary to you sounds extraordinary to me. It's a future to dream for.

Lloyd

No matter how old I get or what I choose to do with my life, I will always want to put on my skates and step onto the ice. I feel as natural and comfortable on my blades as most people do in an old pair of slippers. They are almost a part of me and I couldn't imagine my life without them, or the cold, glassy surface I glide, spin, and jump on.

In March of 1999, Isabelle and I were invited to take part in an event in Toronto called "A Legendary Night of Figure Skating." To celebrate the passing of the torch from the old Maple Leaf Gardens to the new Air Canada Centre, Canadian figure skating champions from all eras gathered together for a unique evening.

As I watched Donald Jackson perform, I couldn't help but reflect that he had won the World Championship in 1962—a full year before I was born. Yet on the ice, he took on the appearance of a young man, still performing the jumps that have made him a legend. Watching him was a truly special experience.

The finale brought skaters of every age and background onto the ice together. Skaters who had been champions more than sixty years ago stood side by side on their skates with the champions of today. At that moment, we all shared a common bond—the pure love of skating.

Isabelle

Unlike almost every other skater I know, I don't think I will need to skate after I leave the sport. If my children wanted to learn, I would take them to the rink and go on the ice with them. Or if my family wanted to spend a day's outing on a frozen pond, I would certainly join them. But I would never go myself.

I still love the basics of skating that drew me to the sport in the first place. To glide across the ice and feel the cold rush of air on my cheeks is a very liberating feeling. And I would miss it. However, I would not put on a pair of skates on a Saturday morning and go to the rink just to feel the pleasure again. I may change my mind someday, but I doubt it. When I move on, it will be for something else that I love. I will savor and remember the enjoyment skating gave me, but I will never look back.

Lloyd

I think the most difficult part of facing retirement will be losing the time Isabelle and I now share. Without the training, the competitions, the shows, and the tours to bring us together, I fear our paths will divide. However, the memories will endure. Isabelle has been my partner and my strength. No matter where life takes the two of us, she will always be my best friend.

Isabelle

Lloyd and I have spent so much time together, and our lives are very much intertwined. I care deeply about him. And I understand that one day we may not see each other as much. But I would always have the need to talk to him—to share my emotions and fears and joys. I can picture my life without skating, but I could never imagine it without Lloyd. To even try would be impossible.

EPILOGUE

Stars on Ice Tour

Toronto, Ontario – April 1999

T HE AIR CANADA CENTRE in Toronto buzzed with excitement. Some of the finest figure skaters in the world were about to step onto the ice and the crowd was eager with anticipation. In the audience, people held signs and wore T-shirts announcing their favorite skaters. Not only were they going to see one of the most highly acclaimed ice shows ever, it was also going to be televised—an added treat to the die-hard figure skating fan.

One by one, the skaters made their entrance on the ice amid the roar of an approving crowd. Kurt Browning, Tara Lipinski, Brian Orser, Steven Cousins, Lu Chen, Josée Chouinard, Meno and Sand, Bourne and Kraatz, and Brasseur and Eisler. Then the talented group performed a number together befitting a Broadway show. With the intricate steps and precise timing they performed, one would think they had been working as a company for months. However, it had only been two weeks since the skaters had met in Halifax to rehearse the show. One week later, it was on the road.

Each of the skaters went on to perform individual numbers. They were all good. Some were great. And then Lloyd and Isabelle stepped onto the ice. The building was suddenly charged with electricity. Everyone in the audience knew they were about to be brought to the edges of their seats.

Lloyd was dressed in black, while Isabelle wore a simple red sweater and black leggings—suitable attire for a team that was better known for dangerous moves than for wearing sequined costumes with flowing sleeves. The music began and Shania Twain's clear voice sang out: *"Looks like we made it. Look how far we've come up baby. Might have took the long way. We knew we'd get there someday."*

The couple began to skate. Faster and faster, they moved around the rink, their timing always perfect and in sync with each other. Then a series of lifts and spins began that caused the audience to hold their breath in fear and delight.

"They said, I bet, they'll never make it. But just look at us holding on. We're still together, going strong." The words from "You're Still the One" were particularly poignant for the couple who had beat the odds. Since Brasseur and Eisler had first come together, there weren't too many in the figure skating world who had faith they could make it as a team. But watching them on this night perform in such harmony, one would think they had been born to skate together.

In between thrilling pairs elements, some recently invented by the couple and as yet unnamed, was a tenderness and intimacy they shared. Lloyd and Isabelle trusted each other in a way that few people do either on or off the ice. The bond was apparent to the audience and only served to endear the couple that had become so familiar to Canadians and figure skating fans worldwide.

When the program ended, Lloyd and Isabelle stood at center ice and took their bows to a standing ovation. Their faces were flushed with satisfaction and joy. With broad smiles, they waved at the crowd, who had come to love them. Through their skating, they had created many glorious memories for all who watched them grow and thrive together. There could be no doubt about it. Brasseur and Eisler were a team that would live on forever.

INDEX